MW00851863

Investing In
Short-Term Rentals

Investing In Short-Term Rentals
The Fast Path To Financial Freedom

Michael Elefante

©2024 All Rights Reserved. No portion of this book may be reproduced, stored in a retrieval system, or transmitted in any form or by any means-electronic, mechanical, photocopy, recording, scanning, or other-except for brief quotations in critical reviews or articles without the prior permission of the author.

Published by Game Changer Publishing

Paperback ISBN: 978-1-963793-89-5
Hardcover ISBN: 978-1-963793-70-3
Digital ISBN: 978-1-963793-71-0

www.GameChangerPublishing.com

DEDICATION

To my wife, Jill.
Without your unwavering support and shared vision…
None of this would have been possible.
Why not us?

Read This First

Just to say thank you for buying and reading my book, I would like to give you a few free bonus gifts, no strings attached!

To Download Your Free Gifts, Scan the QR Code:

Investing In Short-Term Rentals

The Fast Path To Financial Freedom

Michael Elefante

www.GameChangerPublishing.com

Foreword

Michael Elefante's story is a testament to the power of savvy investing and strategic thinking in the world of short-term rentals (STRs). Alongside his wife, Jill, Michael has not just built a seven-figure short-term rental empire; he's charted a course for others to follow suit. Michael's new book captures the essence of his approach: clear, data-driven, and remarkably effective.

What excites me, as the CEO of AirDNA, is seeing our analytics turned into the kind of actionable knowledge that Michael has leveraged so skillfully. I am deeply gratified to see our platform's data harnessed to such a powerful effect. This book does more than just talk about success—it shows you the nuts and bolts of smart STR investing, using real-world data to find and unlock profitable ventures. Michael's practical use of our platform highlights just how accessible and impactful data can be when applied with intent and intelligence.

As you turn these pages, prepare to be equipped with a profound understanding of market analysis, investment strategies, and the art of competitive differentiation. Through Michael's insights and effective use of AirDNA's data, the details of successful STR investing come into sharp focus. Whether you're a seasoned investor or just starting out, Michael's narrative is both an invaluable guide and an inspiring account of what's possible when data-driven decisions meet opportunity.

– Demi Horvat, CEO of AirDNA

Table of Contents

What Is True Financial Freedom?

While my life looks drastically different today than when I began my journey toward financial freedom in 2019, I feel like I come from a place that most young adults (and anyone else working a 9–5) can relate to. I grew up in Chapel Hill, NC, in a stable household with two brothers and two loving parents who worked very hard to support and raise our family. I was an athlete growing up, and all I ever wanted was to pursue professional baseball. School was relatively easy for me, allowing me to maintain As and Bs throughout grade school. After graduating high school in 2011, I enrolled at Elon University on a baseball scholarship. However, in the fall of my sophomore year of college, I suffered an elbow injury during practice, resulting in a medical redshirt for the spring season. Despite this setback, I continued my education and graduated from Elon University in May 2015 with a bachelor's degree in finance. I was hoping to get selected in the Major League Baseball draft and have the opportunity to play professionally. But I knew that if I didn't get drafted, I would have the option to go back for a fifth year and utilize my last year of NCAA eligibility. Spoiler alert: I did not get drafted, and I was forced to make the decision to opt in for a fifth year of college baseball or enter the workforce full-time.

At this point, I started to weigh my options seriously. I quickly found out how difficult it was to find a good job right out of school. Even though I had a 3.4 GPA from one of the top business schools in the Southeast, I found myself applying for many internships and jobs after I had graduated. Finding little success in entering the workforce, I decided to go back for another year of college baseball. The job I held during the summer of 2015 helped confirm this decision. I started working for a startup company selling a product to medical practices in South Florida. In fact, I was pre-selling a product that wasn't even in production yet. This was a commission-only gig, and I had zero guidance or mentorship. To this day, it remains the worst job I've ever had. I went door to door in 100-degree heat in Jupiter, FL, making exactly zero deals and earning nothing in commission.

The harsh reality set in. I had no money and quickly realized I would have to apply for a second job to help pay for my basic living expenses until I returned to Elon that fall. After applying to dozens of places, I became desperate. The only two companies that interviewed me were Dunkin Donuts and Chipotle. Sitting in those interviews, I couldn't help but think, "What am I doing with my life?" I have a finance degree from a prestigious business school, and on paper, I was more qualified than the managers interviewing me. Yet there I was, competing with high school kids interviewing for the same jobs. Chipotle didn't hire me, so I ultimately accepted the offer from Dunkin Donuts, finding myself pouring coffees at 5:30 in the morning for $7.50 an hour, then doing door-to-door sales for the rest of the day. In the evenings, I would go to a local baseball training facility to get my workouts in. This was far from the life I had envisioned for myself. However, I decided to continue pursuing my passion for baseball. I returned to Elon University, and in May 2016, I left Elon and the game of baseball for the final time.

My passion for baseball was a driving force in my life. It was what I excelled at. I woke up every single day thinking about it and worked hard for it every day. It gave me a sense of purpose. Then, in what seemed like the blink of an eye, it was gone. Suddenly, I was without direction or passion. This was a very difficult time for me. I truly believe that many young people, especially those in their early 20s fresh out of school, struggle with this very situation. They just don't know what to do or how to change it.

So, I did what everyone does. I started applying for jobs. After many applications, I finally landed an entry-level sales position with Sirius Computer Solutions in Dallas, TX. When I started, I had a general understanding of what the job entailed but knew nothing about technology or any of the solutions the company offered its customers.

I remember my first day on the job, being walked to a gray cubicle with a laptop and a landline phone on it. I was told to go online and get sales certifications for the various companies we sold products for. Within two weeks, I was cold-calling between 70 and 100 strangers every single day. My role was simply to set up a meeting with one of our sales reps. Cold-calling is not for the faint of heart. I would have my teeth kicked in every day just for the sake of setting an appointment for someone else who would ultimately earn the commission from selling a product and make the company and its owners rich.

Day after day, I drove home from that job, sitting in traffic in the Dallas heat. For the first time in my life, I was numb; I felt absolutely nothing. Here I was, a college grad in my early 20s, at the beginning of what should have been an exciting time. During those long commutes, I realized something: we spend our lives working. We're conditioned to work hard in school, secure a good job, and then finally work our ass off to earn a "good living" for the next 40+ years. This wasn't my idea of a good life. In fact, it was a very rude awakening for me and my first taste of what's known as "the rat race." My outlook on life became very dismal.

However, this scenario plays out for many, and it was my reality at the time. I was earning $35,000 a year, sitting for long hours in a bland cubicle, calling people I didn't know or care about to set appointments for a company that made no significant impact on my life aside from my meager wages. When I first took this job, my salary of $35,000 a year sounded like a lot of money. However, taxes and retirement accounts were taking a large chunk out of my pocket, and I found myself barely able to pay rent and basic living expenses. I was unable to afford any luxuries such as gym memberships or eating out. I didn't have any additional income aside from this job. Doing what society tells us, I decided to work harder and longer. I really started to embrace the daily grind, hoping a promotion would be around the corner and I would be able to ease off a bit once I got one.

At the end of 2016, I got the promotion and earned a base salary of $48,000, with the potential to make up to $70,000 in total compensation through commission. Although I was making more money and my financial stress had eased up, I still was left feeling as though I needed to do more—make more. My level of happiness hadn't increased; I was still under the illusion that working longer hours and putting in more effort would lead to this elusive happiness that I was seeking. So, I took a second job, working weekends at a winery. Juggling the two jobs, I found myself working seven days a week. After about a year as an inside sales representative for Sirius Computer Solutions, I felt I had reached my income limit. Despite this, I maintained the belief that if I just made more money and worked for a different company, perhaps I would be happier.

In December 2017, after extensive networking and dozens of interviews, I secured a position as an inside sales representative at Google.

I thought to myself, *I have officially "made it,"* landing a job at one of the most desirable companies to work at in the world. At 25, I was earning close to $100,000 per year. Growing up, I had always thought that making $100,000 per year was the pinnacle of what I considered to be rich, and I figured I would be set for life. One of my goals in college was to make $100,000 a year by age 30, so being five years ahead of schedule felt like a significant accomplishment.

Working at Google was incredible. The company provides all the amenities and benefits an employee could possibly desire—free breakfast, lunch, coffee, snacks, a beautiful office, a vibrant workplace, friendly coworkers, excellent 401(k) match, and health benefits. But after a few months at this new job, that familiar numb feeling returned. I found myself going through the motions every day, feeling like a hamster on a wheel. I began to realize that more money didn't bring me an equivalent increase in happiness or fulfillment. I knew I needed a change, but I didn't know what that change would be yet.

In my spare time, I started watching YouTube videos, reading books, and listening to podcasts to learn about real estate, passive income, and financial freedom. I became obsessed with concepts such as figuring out a way to replace my active income with passive income so I wouldn't have to work at a job I hated. This concept sounded amazing, but I wondered how it was possible for someone like me. After exploring various passive income avenues, real estate seemed the most logical.

There are many ways to get started in real estate: house flipping, wholesaling, long-term rentals, multifamily, commercial real estate, etc. I had the misconception that I would need a ton of money to get started. So, in order to get started sooner, and since my income at Google was going to be relatively capped for the next several years in the role I was in, in September 2018, I decided to start looking for a new job again. By October

2018, I had landed a position as an outside sales representative at Extreme Networks in Nashville, TN, with target earnings of $200,000 per year. This opportunity doubled my income potential: it was more money than I had ever imagined making. Yet, I recognized it was a means to an end—I needed to achieve financial freedom and escape the 9–5 grind as quickly as humanly possible.

Before moving to Nashville, I visited the city with my girlfriend at the time, now my wife, Jill, to look for a part of the town we wanted to live in. After considering hotels and rentals, we ultimately chose to stay at an Airbnb in the city. We spent several hundred dollars for a couple of days in a tiny apartment. I started to do the math: *If they are charging this much per night, and renting it out for 20–25 days per month, they have got to be making a killing!* I knew nothing about short-term rentals at the time, but I was intrigued.

I spent the next year studying short-term rentals while we saved up as much money as we could. Short-term rentals seemed the most viable option for me, offering higher cash flow potential than traditional long-term rentals, meaning I could replace my income faster with this strategy. By the end of 2019, we finally built up enough courage and savings to invest in our first short-term rental property in Nashville, TN. We barely had enough for the down payment and closing costs. We came to the stark realization we didn't have any money left to furnish the property, so I sold my truck to buy the necessary furniture.

We closed on the property in October 2019, and by mid-December, we had listed it on Airbnb. It took a few months to gain traction, but by March, we had approximately $13,000 in bookings for a single month, with $7,000 of that as our cash flow! I thought to myself, *This is insane! Why isn't everyone doing this?* The cash flow from this one property was about to cover all our living expenses, and then some, for the month of March. I began to wonder if this was normal or if I was onto something too good to be true.

Then, spring 2020 happened. COVID-19 hit, and panic ensued. Sadly, most of our March reservations were canceled. In fact, we had about $42,000 in future reservations canceled in the following weeks as all major cities began to shut down. Although I was crushed, I wasn't discouraged. I probably felt more optimistic than most people during this period.

In April 2020, my wife and I decided to go all-in on short-term rentals. Eager to quit our jobs as fast as possible and increase our cash flow, we liquidated my 401(k) and her IRA to purchase our second short-term rental property in Nashville. We launched this property on Airbnb in May 2020.

Now, although tourism in Nashville was slow for the remainder of 2020, travel began to pick back up towards the year's end. Surprisingly, we remained cash flow positive from those two properties throughout 2020. We continued saving money from our sales jobs and all our cash flow, aiming for our third property. I had a few big commission checks come in during the summer, and I saved every penny of it.

In September 2020, we purchased our third short-term rental in Gatlinburg, Tennessee, where travel was booming at the time, with everybody looking to be secluded in nature and get out of cities. This property was immediately successful. In November 2020, we profited over $14,000 in a single month from our three short-term rental properties, and in December, the profit exceeded $20,000. I was in utter shock. Just one year after buying our first short-term rental property, we had achieved financial freedom. At this point, we were looking to quit our jobs as soon as possible but decided to add one more property to our portfolio before pulling the plug.

In January 2021, we made it happen. Without any cash left, we got creative and partnered with another couple for our fourth property, splitting the investment and responsibilities 50/50. To finance our half, we did a cash-out refinance on our primary residence. This property, also located in Gatlinburg, TN, needed extensive rehab, which we completed before renting it out in April 2021. By then, tourism had mostly recovered in Nashville, and our four short-term rentals were crushing it. All four properties combined were averaging $30,000 per month in cash flow. That's what we took home after paying the mortgage and all other expenses each month. The $30,000 of monthly cash flow was far more than we needed to pay for our lifestyle. This was our first taste of true financial freedom and abundance, and to this day, it remains the most liberating feeling I have ever experienced. I no longer felt numb; I felt alive. And, at that moment, in April 2021, my wife and I decided to quit our jobs and said goodbye to the rat race—forever.

After quitting our jobs, we rented out our primary home in Nashville as a long-term rental (since we couldn't secure a short-term rental permit for that location) and bought a camper van. We decided to do something we have wanted to do for years: travel around the country like nomads. No job, no boss, no stress, no PTO requests. Just steady income, minimal expenses, and absolute freedom. True freedom.

And that is exactly what we did for the next year. We visited over 20 national parks, hiked more than 400 miles, and lived life on our own terms, all while earning tens of thousands of dollars per month in profit from our short-term rental property investments. We worked just a couple of hours a week from our phones in a camper van. The first month we hit over $50,000 in net cash flow was July 2021, just 1.5 years after making our first investment in real estate and short-term rentals. From just four short-term rental properties, we profited over $50,000 in a single month. It is a moment that I will never forget. Sitting in our camper van outside Glacier

National Park, tallying up all the reservations for the month, we were still in shock. We were traveling full time, yet making more money than we had ever dreamed of.

Fast forward to 2023, we had scaled to seven short-term rental properties, marking the first year we exceeded $1,000,000 in gross rental income.

In short, my wife Jill and I achieved financial freedom at the ripe old age of 27, quitting our jobs a mere 16 months after our first real estate investment. While we had initially set a ten-year goal to become financially free, we reached this milestone just one year into our journey with short-term rental investments. Within three years of our first purchase, we expanded our real estate portfolio to over $7.5M. It consisted of just seven high-quality short-term rental properties that generated over $1M in revenue per year. I found what worked in the industry and used that knowledge to found and operate BNB Investor Academy, a hands-on coaching and mentorship business, teaching others how to get started in short-term rentals. I've had the pleasure of teaching thousands of people how to find, invest in, design, set up, and manage short-term rental properties effectively, becoming one of the industry's most renowned educators and biggest influencers on social media.

But I didn't stop there. Seeing potential in other areas of the industry, I co-founded one of the fastest-growing property management companies in history, Home Team Vacation Rentals, with one of my former students, Elliott Caldwell. We scaled to over 300 properties under management within the first 1.5 years of launching the business. Additionally, I co-own Somerled Designs with Brianna West and Jordan McDonough, a company that has quickly become the fastest-growing and one of the most respected short-term rental design companies in the United States. In its first full year of operation in 2023, Somerled Designs completed over 150 designs for short-term rental homeowners.

That is the power of short-term rentals. They led us to financial freedom and a life of abundance. Today, my wife and I do what we want, when we want, without the stress of working a 9–5 job. And if we can do it, so can you.

What Is True Financial Freedom?

Many people mistake financial stability for financial freedom. Financial stability means that your income, at a minimum, covers your living expenses, such as mortgage or rent, car payments, food, etc. A well-paying job can provide financial stability. Financial freedom, on the other hand, is having enough money saved up, or passive income from your investments, to pay for your lifestyle for the remainder of your life without needing to trade your time for money (aka, having a job).

Financial stability does not equal financial freedom. Why is this? Consider what would happen if you were suddenly fired from your job or if the business you work for went under. How long could you survive before you ran out of money? One week? One month? One year? For most people, surprisingly, the answer is just one to three months, covered by their personal savings or a "rainy day fund."

Sadly, society has it backward. From a young age, we are conditioned to trade all of our time for a better future that is not guaranteed. We wake up and go to school five days per week. We sit, listen, perform tasks, do homework, and if we do well enough, we're able to move up to the next level. The same thing happens year after year until we graduate. Nowadays, you can barely submit a job application for most entry-level jobs without a college degree on your resume. Our society has made it the norm that once you graduate high school, you are expected to go to college for four years. For most people, going to college means moving out of the house you grew up in and becoming a little more independent from your parents.

We go to our classes, where we sit, listen, perform tasks, and do homework. If we do well enough, we graduate and apply for a job. The entirety of our education is focused on creating a good resume for future employers. It signifies how good of a job we do at showing up on time and doing what we are told to do each day.

After college, most people start job hunting. Entering the workforce, they get their first dose of the world's most addictive drug—a paycheck. From an early age, society ingrains the belief that the harder you work and the more hours you put in, the more money you will make in the future. Meanwhile, you're encouraged to slowly invest in a 401(k) or some other retirement savings plan. While investing in a 401(k) is better than not investing at all, it's unlikely to provide you with financial freedom at a young age. Such investment vehicles typically yield average results and rely on compound interest that takes decades to mature before you can benefit from it. All the while, fund managers profit from your money. Society tells us that we need to work until the age of 65–70 years old. Why is that the specific age designated for retirement? Why do we just accept this as the norm? By slowly investing in something like a 401(k), there's really no 100% guarantee that you're going to have the exact amount of money that you need at a specified retirement age in order to live comfortably for the remainder of your life.

The typical retirement age in the United States is between 65 and 70 years old. By then, we should have enough saved up to retire and finally live our lives on our own terms. However, life expectancy in the United States in 2022, according to the CDC, was only 76 years, down from 77 years in 2021. I'm sure you see where I'm going with this, but let me paint the morbid picture for you: We will go to school from a young age, typically from age five to 18. Then, most of us go to college, finishing at around the age of 22 or 23. Some pursue further education, earning graduate degrees or becoming lawyers or doctors, which involves an additional two to six years of schooling. By this point, we've been trading our time for knowledge for nearly 20 years of our lives. Immediately after this, most of us find a 9–5 job and work for the next 40–45 years, trading time for money until we're around 65 or 70 years old. Meanwhile, we have an average life expectancy of around 76 years. Do the math: That only gives 6–11 years for the average person to enjoy retirement before they die. Seems backward, doesn't it?

Money won't buy you happiness, but it can buy you more time to pursue things in life that do bring you happiness. This can be accomplished if, and only if, that money is invested correctly. So, how do we achieve financial freedom at a younger age? To become financially free, you have to generate recurring monthly income that does not directly depend on how you spend your time. The term "passive income" is often overused these days, and most forms of income are never 100% passive. However, the more passive your income, the better.

There are three stages of financial freedom:

Financial Freedom Stage 1: Your investment income, which is mostly passive, completely covers your living expenses indefinitely. This means the level of passive income received each month equals or exceeds your monthly living expenses. If you are already at Stage 1, congratulations—you have technically achieved financial freedom. You no longer depend on a job to financially support yourself or your family.

Financial Freedom Stage 2: Your investment income, which is mostly passive, significantly exceeds your monthly living expenses, providing ample disposable income to reinvest or spend as you wish. At this stage, you can begin to enhance your lifestyle, invest further to grow your passive income, travel more, etc.

Financial Freedom Stage 3: You now have *"fuck you money,"* but in a good way! Your investment income, which is mostly passive, not only covers your living expenses but also leaves you with more than enough disposable income to do what you want, when you want. You're able to pay for your parents or loved ones to retire, treat your friends and family, contribute to charitable causes that matter to you, and fulfill any other of your heart's desires. At this stage, you are able to live a life beyond your wildest imagination.

Let's explore what financial freedom looks like for you. I want you to pause and think about the three stages of financial freedom. Grab a piece of paper or use your phone for notes. At the top, write *"Financial Freedom Plan."* Then, divide it into three sections: *"Stage 1, Stage 2, and Stage 3."*

Stage 1: This step is straightforward. We need to identify our "financial freedom" number. If you maintain a personal budget, you should already know what your Stage 1 financial freedom number is. How much money do you need each month to cover your mortgage or rent, car, food, healthcare needs, etc.? Write this number down. For most people, doing this exercise for the first time is somewhat surprising. You realize how little we actually need to live comfortably. Once financially free, you can spend your time as you please. What would you do with your time each day if you didn't have to work your 9–5 job? Write these activities down. Manifest your vision of what your days will look like. Let's say this number is $5,000 per month. While this is a solid starting point, I encourage you to think even bigger. Let's move on to Stage 2.

Stage 2: Imagine how your life would change if you were earning $10,000 per month in passive income. What about $20,000 or $30,000 per month? At this stage, you are living very comfortably. Write down all the things you would like to do if you were earning $30,000 per month *and* no longer needed to work 40+ hours per week. Manifest this. How would you spend your time? Where would you vacation? What car would you drive? What would your house look like? Although earning $30,000 per month in passive income may seem like a fantasy for most people, it's closer within your reach than you may think. Let's move on to Stage 3, where you'll need to dig deeper and think outside the box.

Stage 3: Imagine what it would feel like if you could donate $100,000 per year to a charity that meant a lot to you without a second thought. That's the level of financial freedom we're aiming for. What would your life look like if you were earning $100,000 per month in passive income? $500,000 per month? $1,000,000 per month? Remember, we're talking about *fuck you money*, but in a good way. Write down what your life looks like at this point. Ask yourself the same questions: How are you spending each day? What does your house look like? What vacations are you taking? What car are you driving? Now, add these questions: *Would you retire your parents? What charitable causes would you like to support in a big way? What dreams could you fulfill for yourself or others?*

Like most new investments or business ventures, 99% of people never take the first step. Additionally, I'm a firm believer that most people don't find success because they don't allow themselves to be successful. Most people shy away at the first sign of adversity. Many also experience imposter syndrome, which is the persistent inability to believe that your success is deserved or has been legitimately achieved through your own efforts or skills. In other words, feeling that you are not capable or worthy of success.

For many years, I experienced imposter syndrome myself. I believe it was one of the main things that prevented me from achieving a higher level of success earlier, whether in college baseball or as a salesman in my prior jobs. I always felt like I wasn't worthy of higher degrees of success and that I held myself back from achieving what I was capable of. It took a great deal of mental effort to manifest what I wanted in life.

If you catch yourself sitting on your couch, seeing financially successful people on TV or social media, and thinking to yourself, *Man, that must be nice.* Well, you'd be right. I'll be the first to tell you, it is really, really nice. It's nice to be financially free. It's nice to not have to worry about money. It's nice to be your own boss. It's nice to wake up on a Monday and for it to feel no different than a Saturday. It's nice to golf or take the boat out on a lake on any random weekday. It's nice to take vacations whenever you'd like without needing permission from an employer. It's nice to retire from the workforce at age 30 instead of 65. My wife and I developed a mantra that has fueled our success over the years.

Initially, we were the couple who envied financially successful people on social media and thought to ourselves, *Must be nice.* Eventually, we shifted our mindset and thought to ourselves, *Why not us? Why shouldn't we achieve financial freedom in our 20s? Why can't we live in our dream home? Why can't we travel the world? Why can't we start a family and build generational wealth?* I encourage you to adopt this same mantra. *Why not you?* Don't fear success. Overcome imposter syndrome. You're capable and deserving of it all.

My passion for and commitment to helping people find their financial freedom are the foundations of this book. Our goals are financial freedom and prosperity, achieved as quickly as possible through short-term rentals. Our hope is that you want it for yourself, too.

CHAPTER ONE

Why Invest in Real Estate: Specifically, Short-Term Rentals?

First and foremost, let's talk about risk. A lot of people assume there are high levels of risk when it comes to investing. Yes, with any investment, there is inherently some level of risk. In fact, I was incredibly risk-averse for many years. I was terrified to lose my hard-earned money. I would not invest much money in the stock market and never thought I would have the courage to invest in real estate because I was so afraid of losing the money that I worked so hard for. Sound familiar?

One day, while driving to Memphis for a client meeting for one of my sales jobs. I had the stark realization that not investing was actually far riskier than investing my money. Think about this for a second: If you are not investing your money, your money is likely just sitting in your bank account, or worse, you spend it. A lot of people feel a false sense of security when their money is sitting in their bank account. Did you know that your money isn't actually sitting at the bank? Banks hold only a fraction of deposits, practicing what is known as "fractional banking." This means that the bank is only required to keep a portion of deposits, and it lends the rest out to its borrowers. The banks are making money off of you.

Secondly, money sitting stagnant and uninvested is losing purchasing power and becoming less valuable over time. This is due to inflation and the Federal Reserve's ability to print new money out of thin air. The United States used to operate on the Gold Standard, which meant that our paper money, the U.S. Dollar, had a value that was directly linked to gold. In 1971, the US came off the Gold Standard, which meant that the Federal Reserve could essentially print money at will. Anytime our country prints money, every single dollar that is circulating throughout the economy becomes worth less and has less buying power than it did the day before. Of course, money is being printed all the time. So, if money is just sitting idle in your bank account, you are technically becoming poorer with each day that goes by.

While your money loses purchasing power, there is actually a far greater risk at hand. Most people only rely on their active income to pay for their living expenses and support their families. So, if your money remains uninvested, you are putting yourself at risk. You will likely spend the majority of your life working a job, trading 40+ hours per week, and chasing a paycheck in the hopes of retiring someday.

Working for an employer may feel safe and secure, but is it truly? At any moment, your employer could let you go and replace you. You are more replaceable than you might think. So, how secure is your job truly? A lot of people harbor a false sense of security with their jobs because they receive a monthly paycheck, have health insurance, and an employer-sponsored 401(k). However, if you were to lose your job tomorrow, how long could you live off your current savings or investments? For most, this period is just one to three months. That, my friends, is risky.

Remember, a job might offer financial stability, but financial stability is not the same as financial freedom. Financial stability means you can comfortably cover your living expenses as long as you're working and earning an adequate income. Financial freedom, on the other hand, means having sufficient ongoing passive income or savings to cover your living expenses without ever needing to rely on a job again. When it comes to financial freedom, money is not the goal; it is just a tool that, if invested correctly, can create a state of financial freedom, granting you complete, unilateral control over your time and how you choose to spend it.

To achieve financial freedom, you first have to dissociate your income from the time you spend working. You need to learn how to make your money work for you. Instead of working for money to pay off the liabilities in your life, you need to take that money and invest in assets that produce monthly cash flow. Let your assets pay for your liabilities.

For many, investing in real estate has always been and likely will always be the simplest path to financial freedom and building wealth. But why is this? It's all about cash flow. To sustain financial freedom, you need cash flow! You invest your money in assets like real estate. The rental income, after deducting the mortgage and other operating expenses, constitutes your cash flow. Once you have enough cash flow to offset your living expenses, you have achieved Stage 1 of financial freedom. While cash flow sets you financially free, it's the equity, depreciation, and appreciation that will truly build your wealth over time. Each month, the mortgage gets paid off by your renters. As your mortgage gets paid off, your equity position in the property grows.

Real estate is a hard asset, meaning it hedges your wealth against inflation and tends to increase in value over time. This is known as appreciation. Historically, home appreciation in the United States has averaged over 4% annually. This means a $100,000 home today, assuming a 4% year-over-year appreciation, would be worth $104,000 next year. This effect compounds over time: in year two, it's worth $108,160; by year five, it's $121,665; in ten years, $148,024; and after 30 years, your initial

$100,000 investment is now worth $324,340. Sounds better than letting your money sit idle in a savings account, doesn't it?

What sets real estate apart as an asset is its depreciation. While the value of real estate generally appreciates over time, the physical structure of any piece of real estate technically depreciates. The IRS deems residential properties to have a useful life of 27.5 years and commercial properties 39 years. Over the course of the specified time period, the depreciation reduces your taxable income. You will ultimately pay far less taxes, if any, on your cash flow from your real estate investments compared to the amount that you're paying on your earned income. This is why real estate is so special. By paying less in taxes, we can invest at a higher frequency. The cash flow will set you financially free, and owning real estate for the long term will make you wealthy.

Now that we have touched on why investing in real estate is so powerful, let's talk about the power of short-term rentals and why I am a true believer that investing in short-term rentals is the fastest path to financial freedom. First of all, any real estate investor should be investing for cash flow. While appreciation, depreciation, and other auxiliary benefits you get from real estate investments are important to consider, cash flow is what is ultimately going to set you financially free. While a long-term rental typically provides a few hundred dollars of monthly cash flow, short-term rentals have the potential to cash flow thousands per month. Let me say that again: a single short-term rental has the potential to cash flow thousands of dollars per month.

When I first explored real estate, I read books, watched YouTube videos, and listened to podcasts. The general rule of thumb was $200 cash flow per door. One of my initial objectives was to build a portfolio generating $10,000 cash flow per month. At $200 per door, achieving this goal would require 50 long-term rentals of equivalent value. That seemed incredibly daunting and like a lot of work to me! I was discouraged, but after learning about short-term rentals, my mindset shifted, and I began to get really excited. An average short-term rental, when set up and managed effectively, typically cash flows between $2,000 and $4,000 per month. *Wow!* So, I would only need three to five average short-term rentals to cash flow $10,000 instead of 50 long-term rentals?

It only takes one to three good short-term rentals to replace most people's 9–5 income. In fact, one great short-term rental can set most people financially free. My smallest property, a two-bedroom condo in Nashville, TN, cash flows an average of $4,000 per month. Would you be able to cover most or all of your basic monthly living expenses with $4,000 per month or $48,000 per year? For most people, the answer is probably yes!

Here's a brief story about Logan and Bri West, two of my first-ever coaching clients at BNB Investor Academy. Bri found my videos on TikTok and shared them with her husband, Logan, encouraging him to look into short-term rentals. Logan was a successful salesman in the pest control industry, and Bri was working in marketing at the time. They lived near Salt Lake City, Utah, with their two young daughters. Although Logan was a higher-income earner, he was tired of working so much. He and Bri both wanted financial freedom so they could spend time with their daughters and do what they were passionate about each and every day, such as golf and travel. Logan had invested in two long-term rentals previously, but they were only providing mediocre cash flow. He was cash-flowing a few hundred dollars per month and recognized the long-term benefits of owning these rentals, but the cash flow wasn't life-changing, and it would take years, if not decades, to replace his income. His goal was to scale his cash flow as quickly as possible. Logan signed up to work with me and my team and was immediately hooked on short-term rentals.

They started off by doing a rental arbitrage deal in Utah. (You'll learn more about rental arbitrage and other strategies in the next chapter.) The investment totaled about $18,000, and they were cash-flowing, net of all expenses and rent, $3,000 to $4,000 per month! That is insane cash flow and return on investment. After seeing this property perform as well as it did, they quickly listed their two long-term rentals for sale and reinvested that money into two more short-term rentals. Within just a few months, the young couple from Utah went from a few hundred dollars per month to over $10,000 per month in cash flow. They accomplished this with just three short-term rentals.

Fast forward to 2023, just two years after starting their short-term rental investing journey: Logan and Bri have scaled to ten properties, which bring in on average $150,000 per month in gross rental income and $60,000 to $75,000 per month in net cash flow.

Bri and Logan didn't pigeonhole themselves into only one strategy or confine themselves to the cash they had sitting in their savings. They started off with just $18,000 on a rental arbitrage deal. They quickly bought two properties, and have since scaled mainly by partnering with other members of the BNB Investor Academy community.

In fact, Logan and Bri have purchased several investments without using any of their own money! One thing I always encourage new investors to think about is this: Instead of asking how much you need to get started, you should be asking yourself how much money you have currently, and pick the best strategy that aligns with your current budget.

To make this possible, let's dig into the different short-term rental investing strategies that you can start today, regardless of your current situation!

You can learn more about BNB Investor Academy by scanning this QR code or visit www.bnbinvestoracademy.com.

CHAPTER TWO

Short-Term Rental Investment Strategies

O ne of the amazing things about short-term rental investments is that you can start now, regardless of your budget. Many investment strategies in the real estate sector are cost-prohibitive for the average person. The beauty of short-term rentals is that you can look at what money you currently have available to you and then, based on that answer, choose which short-term rental investment strategy to start with. We will cover each of these strategies in depth and discuss the pros and cons of each.

Let's start with what most of you think about when it comes to investing in real estate, and that is to actually buy a property. I call this method "Buy and Hold."

Buy and Hold

Typically, a "buy and hold" strategy requires a down payment. Without creative financing, you're likely going to need to put down 10%–20% of the purchase price. This can be cost-prohibitive for many new investors. For instance, a 20% down payment on a $500,000 property amounts to $100,000, a sum beyond the reach of many starting out. On top of that, you will need to pay closing costs, which usually range from 3% to 6% of the loan amount.

One advantage you have when buying real estate is leverage. You do not have to buy a property all-cash. You can leverage the bank's money and put down, for example, 20%, and leverage the other 80% of the purchase price from the bank in order to acquire the asset. Leverage is a powerful tool if used correctly. Instead of purchasing one property all-cash, you could buy four to five properties at the same price point by utilizing leverage. The return on investment typically increases when leveraging multiple properties instead of buying just one all-cash.

Let's dive into the financial benefits of owning real estate, starting with cash flow. The rental income you receive each month, minus your mortgage and operating expenses, constitutes your cash flow. As we've noted previously, it's crucial to remember that cash flow is key to achieving financial freedom. Although a mortgage is considered an expense in cash flow calculations, part of the mortgage payment (unless it's an interest-only loan) covers interest to the bank, and the rest is the principal being paid down on the loan. You get to keep 100% of that principal pay down, which builds your equity position in that asset over the long term. Ultimately, once the mortgage is fully paid off, you own the property free and clear, with your renters having effectively paid off the mortgage for you!

As we noted above, real estate increases in value over time, a phenomenon known as appreciation. This is what makes leverage so powerful. Although you're putting down only 20% on a property, you still capture 100% of its appreciated value. For example, if you buy a $500,000 property and put down 20%, that is $100,000 invested. Let's say, in five years, that property is now worth $600,000. Although you only put down 20%, you get to keep 100% of the $100,000 worth of appreciation! Guess what? If you bought the property in cash and paid $500,000, you'd still keep the same $100,000.

Let's calculate the difference in ROI (Return on Investment), just by looking at appreciation between buying with leverage vs. buying cash. We calculate this by dividing the appreciation amount of $100,000 by the amount of cash invested. If you bought cash, you'd simply take the $100,000 of appreciation divided by the $500,000 cash invested, equaling a 20% ROI. On the other hand, when using leverage and putting just 20% down, you would take the $100,000 of appreciation and divide it by the $100,000 cash invested, which is a 100% ROI. By using leverage, you could hypothetically buy five similar properties instead of buying one all-cash. If you did buy five properties, and they all appreciated the same $100,000 amount, you'd have gained $500,000 in equity from appreciation, instead of only $100,000 by buying one property all-cash. That's the power of leverage.

You can increase the rate of appreciation on a property further by doing some sort of rehab. This could be accomplished by adding additional bedrooms, remodeling the bathrooms or the kitchen, replacing old carpet with new hardwood floors, etc. Not only are you forcing appreciation to the property, but you are also making it a more attractive short-term rental. By investing in the right things, you will be able to rent it out for more per night, be booked at a higher occupancy rate, and increase the value of the property.

One of the most powerful aspects of buying and owning real estate isn't the cash flow or appreciation. It's the depreciation. According to the IRS, depreciation is an annual income tax deduction that allows you to recover the cost or other basis of a certain property over the time you use the property. It is an allowance for the wear and tear, deterioration, or obsolescence of the property. In other words, you are able to deduct the depreciation of your property to effectively reduce your taxable income on your cash flow— or, in some cases, eliminate it altogether.

While the buy-and-hold strategy offers many advantages, it also has its drawbacks. The most significant is the higher cost barrier to entry compared to other strategies. You have to fork out a sizable down payment in most cases, pay for closing costs, spend money on rehab if necessary, and ultimately design and furnish the property. Because of this, scaling takes more money and time if you're doing it with your own capital.

Although buying property may be cost-prohibitive for most new investors, I strongly encourage you to find people to partner with on deals. Leverage other people's money (OPM). In fact, you may be surprised to hear that most real estate investors that scale the fastest are, in fact, leveraging other people's money, not their own. You can tap into your network and relationships with individuals who have capital to invest but lack the time or knowledge to do the work themselves, such as finding properties, setting them up, and managing them. While they bring the money to the table, you bring the expertise and hustle. By leveraging other people's money, you can scale much faster.

Begin with your current network. You'd be surprised how easy it actually is to find people with money who are willing to partner on deals. Start with family or friends, then branch out to your wider network or even strangers. The one mistake I see a lot of people make is simply going around asking if someone wants to be their real estate partner without bringing a specific deal to the conversation. A far more effective strategy is to first find properties that make great investments and then present those properties and the investment breakdown to potential investment partners. A great way to pitch this is to ask them if they know anyone in their network who would be interested in partnering on this deal with you. If they have the capital themselves, they will most likely not suggest someone they know but, instead, ask if they can partner with you!

Rental Arbitrage

Let's say you have a little bit of money saved up but not enough to purchase a property. One of the best strategies for starting and scaling very quickly with short-term rentals is rental arbitrage.

In a nutshell, rental arbitrage is simply renting a property from someone else and then subletting it out as a short-term rental (with permission from the landlord to sublet it out on a short-term basis). Why is this strategy so powerful? More often than not, you don't need to have credit, and you only need to have enough money for furniture and any costs associated with setting up the lease, such as a security deposit, the first month's rent, and an application fee. But there is no down payment or closing costs, as there would be if you were buying a property. Because the capital investment required for rental arbitrage is far lower than purchasing a property, the cash-on-cash return is typically much higher. We will delve into key investing metrics, such as cash-on-cash return, later. A well-executed rental arbitrage deal can yield a cash-on-cash return well north of 100%, and often 200%–300% if you are highly skilled.

If you're starting with less than $50,000, I strongly recommend pursuing rental arbitrage, as it allows you to begin and scale your cash flow much faster. Consider this example to understand how you can scale starting with $10,000. Suppose in the first month, you secure a property for $10,000 all-in. This includes lease costs, furniture, and any other setup expenses.

This property could generate a cash flow of $1,000 per month. After ten months, assuming you are using no additional income or savings, you'll have $10,000 in the bank to reinvest. You can then acquire a second property with the same setup costs of $10,000. Now, with two properties, your average monthly cash flow is $2,000. After another five months, you'll have another $10,000 to invest. You see where I'm going with this. If you do the math, by month 21, you should own five properties with a monthly cash flow of around $5,000. At this stage, you can start to scale to larger units that may require more investment in furniture, etc., but have the potential to generate significantly higher monthly cash flow. As you acquire more properties, you'll become more efficient in setting them up and managing them. Reaching a net cash flow of $10,000 per month, starting with just $10,000, is more attainable than you might think.

In addition to using other people's money to purchase real estate, you can apply the same approach to rental arbitrage. One of my BNB Investor Academy mentees, Ben, was a 22-year-old college student with no money, working an unpaid internship that later became a full-time job. He was surrounded by colleagues who were earning high incomes. Ben evaluated properties for rental arbitrage and presented his analysis to one of his colleagues at the company. Initially, the gentleman didn't believe that he would get a 100%+ ROI with a small studio apartment in Charlotte, NC, through rental arbitrage. However, after Ben explained the model and shared the investment analysis, including projections, local comps, and so on, the investor decided to commit $10,000. The property consistently outperformed their cash flow expectations, and they quickly proceeded to set up a second rental arbitrage unit together. The takeaway from this story is that if a 22-year-old college student with no money and an unpaid internship can succeed in rental arbitrage, so can you!

The advantages of rental arbitrage are clear: You can start with less money, you can scale much faster than buying, and your cash-on-cash return will be higher because there is no down payment or closing costs. However, there are some downsides. With rental arbitrage, you have less control over the property itself because you do not own it. Often, you cannot make substantial changes to the property to alter its appearance or upgrade certain aspects to make it more attractive to renters. Additionally, since you are renting via a lease agreement, you take the risk of the lease expiring and the landlord not renewing with you or increasing rent each year. If they do not renew, you now have a bunch of furniture you paid for that you need to either sell or find a new property to put it in.

If you got a 100% return on your investment doing rental arbitrage during year one, but your lease expired, and you cannot renew, you basically just did a whole bunch of work to have renters pay for furniture and the cost of your lease for a year. It's, therefore, a good idea to include provisions in your lease to allow you to rent for multiple years or have the option to renew. If rent increases year over year, which it typically does in most markets, this can also dampen your cash flow in years to come if daily rates do not also increase with your short-term rental. The other downside to rental arbitrage is that there is no equity and no depreciation, unlike owning property. Each month, as a renter, you are paying off the mortgage for the homeowner, and they reap the benefits of any appreciation and depreciation of the property, not you.

Lastly, with rental arbitrage, it can be a challenge to get a landlord to agree to let you do this in the first place! This is, in fact, the most challenging aspect of rental arbitrage and what deters people early on from starting. The problem is that most people simply just email or call a landlord and ask them if they can rent their property and do Airbnb. This will get you a resounding no 99.99% of the time! You need to understand how to pitch landlords and, more importantly, how to create a "win-win" relationship with them. You must explain to the landlord that renting to you is better than renting to a typical tenant. Why is this? For starters, ask the landlord what their biggest yearly expense is. The answer is likely vacancy and turnover. When units sit vacant, the landlord and homeowner lose rental income and incur costs. If nobody is paying rent, they still have to pay the mortgage, utility bills, and any other costs associated with holding that unit vacant.

Additionally, it costs money to fill the unit with a new tenant! They have to advertise the unit, clean it, paint it, and do whatever else necessary to get it in rent-ready condition again. Higher vacancy equals less profit for the landlord and homeowner. By renting to you instead of a normal tenant, you will essentially eliminate their vacancy costs because as long as you are profitable, you are going to rent it for years to come, not just 6–12 months.

Another big issue with typical renters is that they truly live in a place, and many people do not clean or maintain the property as if it were their own. If rented to you, in order to maintain positive reviews on Airbnb, you have to keep the property in impeccable condition and professionally cleaned between each group of guests. This means the property will stay in rent-ready and for-sale condition, which will hold the resale value better.

To convince a landlord to allow you to do rental arbitrage, you have to ensure they are financially incentivized and understand the benefits of renting to you versus someone else. If you can accomplish this, you will be surprised at how many landlords will be open to renting to you!

Abby, one of my students at BNB Investor Academy, was making $3,000 per month cash flow on her first rental arbitrage deal, a studio apartment in Nashville, Tennessee. Abby had no prior experience, and she only had about $15,000 to $20,000 of money to invest starting out. Although she was unable to purchase a property, she learned about rental arbitrage and quickly went all-in on the strategy. Within the first three months of launching her first listing, she was cash-flowing, on average, $3,000 per month. Remember, cash flow is what she took home after paying rent and all other expenses! And she was achieving a 300%-plus return on her investment! Abby scaled to three arbitrage properties within the first two years and is actively working to scale her portfolio further. If Abby can do it, so can you!

Co-Hosting and Property Management

Now, let's say you have absolutely no money, but you're very keen on getting started in short-term rentals. Instead of waiting and saving up for multiple years, what I would encourage you to do is try to build and foster a relationship with homeowners or investors so you can begin a co-hosting or professional property management business. The biggest benefit here is that very little, or no money is required to begin co-hosting properties.

When you manage a short-term rental for someone else, you manage the listing and reservations, you communicate with guests and cleaners, and you run the day-to-day operations. You make money by charging a management fee, which is most frequently calculated as a percentage of the revenue the property generates each month. The typical property management fee in the short-term rental industry is 20%–25% of revenue. Let's look at an example. If you manage a property that does $120,000 gross revenue per year and you charge a 20% management fee, that is $24,000 per year or $2,000 per month! If you have five properties under management of similar caliber, you are making $10,000 per month. If you have ten properties, that's $20,000 per month. But I encourage you to think bigger.

Imagine if you scale to 100 properties under management; that would be $200,000 a month in gross income minus your expenses. Of course, if you scale to 100 properties, you will likely hire multiple people to help run the day-to-day operations and guest communications. Property management has the potential to be hyper-scalable and profitable if done right. There are so many old property management companies out there that do a disservice to their homeowners. Many of them still operate primarily on old direct booking sites with outdated marketing tactics or none at all. They don't use dynamic pricing strategies, and they do not leverage technology to automate their business operations. Many of them charge upwards of 30%–35% of revenue as their property management fee, which is outrageously expensive, in my opinion. This typically leaves homeowners with little or no profit at all. This presents a great opportunity for you to manage for the same or a lower management fee and produce higher revenue than these companies are currently doing for their homeowners.

One of the biggest benefits of owning a property management company is that you can eventually sell the business for a multiple of EBITDA (earnings before interest, taxes, depreciation, and amortization), which is typically how property management companies are valued. Other property management companies or private equity groups purchase smaller management companies all the time because it is easier to scale by buying than it is to grow organically. If you grow your business sustainably, you could potentially have a big payday in the future!

There are a few downsides to property management. As you scale, you truly have to treat this as a formal business and hire the right employees. If you don't, you will hit some major roadblocks and bottlenecks. You also do not own any of the real estate yourself, so you don't get the benefits there either. You are at the mercy of the homeowners and what they are willing to spend money on. This means that if a property needs an updated design in order to compete in a market, but the homeowner refuses to spend the money on proper design and furniture, you are stuck with the property as is.

Co-hosting and property management are different. The key distinction between the two is as follows: with co-hosting, you are technically helping a homeowner manage their property, and you bill them at the end of each month for your fee. With property management, you provide full-service property management and are responsible for collecting all payments from guests, paying for the cleaners and maintenance, and remitting homeowner distributions each month. While co-hosting is a great way to start out, pivoting to full-blown property management is the way to go long-term if you want to scale beyond just a few properties under management.

Here's a quick story about one of my first students to ever join BNB Investor Academy. Elliott Caldwell joined the program in early 2021. He bought a few properties by himself and then partnered on a few deals with another investor. He scaled to six properties within the first year and then realized that in the markets he was operating in, he was outperforming the neighbors—by a lot. He started networking with the owners of those properties and told them how much he was making with his properties down the street. Many of them were in disbelief. Elliott showed them the revenue numbers and active reservations on Airbnb and Vrbo. Within weeks, those homeowners fired their property managers and signed contracts with Elliott to manage instead. Elliott quickly scaled to 20 properties under management and eventually approached me to partner with him to formalize the business. Elliott's co-hosting business was the foundation of what became Home Team Vacation Rentals, which, as of 2024, was one of the fastest-growing nationwide property management companies in the USA. Within the first year and a half, Home Team Vacation Rentals scaled to over 300 properties under management! The focus of Home Team Vacation Rentals has always been to maximize revenue and cash flow for homeowners, and we have done this very successfully. We believe this is the main reason we have been able to scale so quickly and effectively.

If you are reading this book and you have one or more properties that are being poorly managed, feel free to scan this QR code or reach out to our team at www.hometeamvr.com.

I love short-term rentals because there are ways to start and scale regardless of your starting budget! Pick a strategy that is right for you and aligns with your goals. You will be surprised at how quickly you can scale your monthly cash flow!

CHAPTER THREE

Market Selection & Creating a "Buy Box"

"Airbnb is oversaturated." Have you heard this before? It's one of the most common remarks I hear. "You were lucky and started at the right time." "It's too competitive now." "Interest rates are too high." "Prices are too high." Let me share a little secret I've learned over the years: There's never a perfect time to buy real estate, and there's never a perfect time to get started in short-term rentals. Was Airbnb less competitive five years ago? Yes, absolutely! Can you still make a killing and achieve insane levels of cash flow and ROI with short-term rentals today? Yes, absolutely! One thing people often forget is that vacation rentals have been around for decades, long before companies like Airbnb came along.

In the past, to find a rental, you had to call property management companies to check availability. Platforms like Airbnb and Vrbo have made it easier to find and book short-term rentals. Remember, people will always travel. People will always take time off from work. People will never stop getting engaged and celebrating a bachelor or bachelorette party. People will never stop getting married. People will never stop taking their family on vacations and creating lifelong memories. People have a natural desire to seek adventure and new experiences. And when people travel, they want the best possible accommodation that fits their budget.

So, if you're just starting your short-term rental investing journey, where do you even begin? It starts with market research. The two most common questions that people ask me are, "What market should I invest in?" and "What is the best market to invest in right now?" While market selection is important, finding the perfect market is not what you should be focused on—because it doesn't exist. Instead, you should be focused on finding the best possible opportunity within a sustainable market. At the end of the day, you want to have a strong cash flow not just in the first one to two years but in ten years and beyond. The problem with trying to find the perfect market is that it does not exist. If it did, everyone would be investing there and nowhere else. Additionally, spinning your wheels searching for the perfect market will quickly become overwhelming, and you will find yourself stuck in this part of the process. This is what keeps 99% of people in analysis paralysis and prevents them from ever investing a dime of their own money. So first, let's cover how to find and evaluate markets, and then we will dive into how to build a "buy box" in a given market.

Generally speaking, there are two types of markets: **vacation markets** and **urban markets.** Traditional **vacation markets**, such as lakes, beaches, and mountains, have hosted short-term rentals for decades. These are destinations where families typically travel and spend an average of three to seven days at a time. Often, vacation markets have lower regulatory barriers compared to urban markets, making them and short-term rentals a natural fit. Tourism is a key support for most of these local economies and is often where most tax revenue is generated. Therefore, many vacation markets tend to be more investor-friendly, and regulation and permit requirements tend to be more lax compared to urban markets. Competition in vacation markets is a mix of older rentals managed by legacy property management companies and a new wave of investors who are updating properties with better design and amenities. When looking for a new market to invest in within traditional vacation areas, there are a few things to keep in mind.

On the one hand, there are drive-to vacation markets where the destination itself is the main attraction. The most sustainable vacation markets to invest in are often the ones within driving distance from one or more large metropolitan areas that are growing in population. What happens when people move to a new city? They look for things to do and new places to explore with their friends and family. They will hop in the car and drive to all the fun vacation spots within a few hours' drive. The more these populations grow, the stronger the demand becomes for nearby vacation markets. For example, the Outer Banks in North Carolina is a popular destination for people from across the East Coast who drive there to rent a beach house for a week during the summer months. They don't spend much time or money outside of just hanging on the beach or by the pool each day. Therefore, the majority of the expenses allocated to their trip are gas, accommodation, and groceries. Most major drive-to vacation destinations, such as the Outer Banks, are within a three- to five-hour drive from one or more major metropolitan areas, such as Raleigh, NC.

Another prime example is the Great Smoky Mountains National Park in Tennessee and North Carolina, the most visited national park in the USA, attracting over 15 million annual visitors. It's located a few hours drive from Nashville, Atlanta, Charlotte, Raleigh, Greenville, and other growing metropolitan areas. The Smokies are another destination that typically doesn't cost too much outside of gas, accommodation, and groceries. There are more things to do there, such as restaurants, activities like Dollywood amusement park, and so on. But for the most part, people want to get their entire family together, rent a big cabin in the mountains, and explore the national park (which doesn't charge an entrance fee, by the way).

On the other hand, you have vacation markets that are harder-to-reach destinations and often come with more expensive activities. These are locations where the activities someone will primarily be participating in cost money. For example, major ski resorts in Colorado and Disney World fall into this category. Most people have to fly to Denver, rent a car to drive to a ski resort, pay for accommodation and lift tickets, and rent or buy ski equipment. People from all over the world fly to Disney World, pay for accommodations, pay for park tickets, pay to eat at the resort or local restaurants, and often pay for other entertainment or activities during their vacation.

Why is it important to differentiate between these types of vacation markets? Well, during economic uncertainty or recessionary periods, people will still travel and go on vacation. However, they are more likely to opt for the less-expensive vacation, which for most people will be the location where they can pile their family into a car and drive to without spending a ton of extra money on activities. They will go to beaches, mountains, and lakes.

The second type of market is **urban markets**. Unlike the traditional vacation markets, urban markets did not have many short-term rentals until the emergence of Airbnb in the early 2010s. Hotels historically dominated most travel accommodations in these cities. Urban markets are typically subject to more regulation and stricter permit requirements than vacation markets. Some cities have been flooded with new short-term rental properties in recent years, making some markets ultra-competitive very quickly. Most cities are cracking down on short-term rental regulation, and some even outright banning short-term rentals.

While many cities have stricter regulations, don't let regulations and permitting alone scare you away from investing in a fruitful market. In some cases, more regulation can be a good thing for investors. Why is this the case? Most regulations revolve around zoning, meaning some areas with residential-zoned properties are not eligible for a non-owner-occupied short-term rental permit. Some cities have occupancy restrictions on the number of people you are allowed to accommodate, according to the number of bedrooms your property has. Some cities simply cap the number of permits they allow. This makes it more challenging and competitive to find a good investment property that is zoned for a non-owner-occupied short-term rental permit.

There are two consequences to this. First, it scares off many investors just because they hear that a city has heavy regulations, so they assume they can't operate a short-term rental there and give up very quickly. Second, it slows down the growth of short-term rental supply in a given market and ultimately can impose what I call a "soft cap" on supply in a market. This is a very good thing for you as an investor! It can help you secure higher daily rates, higher occupancy, and ultimately higher revenue, not just today, but long-term. In a market with no regulation, supply can shoot up very quickly, which will lower the RevPAR (revenue per available rental) and cause diminishing returns for short-term rental investors.

While you can make money in most urban markets, there are a few key criteria I look for when considering one as a place to invest.

First, the city currently has steady tourism and, ideally, experiences year-over-year growth in tourist numbers. Why do people visit the city? Are they traveling solo or in large groups? Are they visiting for one-night stays, or are they vacationing here and staying for three-plus days? Is the city growing in popularity on social media?

Two, is the city's population growing? Population growth is an important factor for short-term rental investors for two reasons. Firstly, a growing population typically means that real estate will appreciate more sustainably in the long term. As businesses and people move into a city, the demand for housing increases, putting pressure on supply in the market and spurring capital investment and growth. This is why cities such as Austin, TX, or Nashville, TN, have seen some of the highest levels of home appreciation and rent increases in the 2010s and 2020s. What do people need when they move their families to a new city? A place to live!

This brings me to my second point: *short-term rentals aren't just for people on vacation.* A family moving across the country to a new city that they have never been to before wants to know what it's like to live there before buying a house of their own. They might rent furnished accommodations for days, weeks, or even months while searching for the perfect home in the ideal zip code to buy. A growing population not only ensures a fruitful long-term investment but will also keep demand strong and growing, which can help keep RevPAR steady or growing as well.

Urban markets offer a unique opportunity to operate properties as both short-term (less than 30 days at a time) and mid-term rentals (more than 30 days at a time). In urban areas, there are several reasons someone might need furnished accommodations for 30–90 days.

1. There are families moving to the area who have either not found a home to buy or are building a home and waiting for it to be finished.

2. You have corporate travel in large and growing cities where executives, contract workers, travel nurses, and other professionals need a place to stay for one to three months at a time.

3. You can work with insurance companies and rent to families through the insurance company for various length contracts.

4. Depending on the location, there may be seasonal travelers who like to spend multiple months per year visiting, such as

"snowbirds" visiting many South Florida markets during the winter and early spring. Being able to operate as a furnished mid-term rental gives you flexibility with your property that most vacation markets do not provide.

Let's go back to market supply for a second. Don't just assume a market is oversaturated and you cannot make any money because you heard on social media that the supply has increased. We need to look deeper than this. There are so many tools to leverage to better understand the data in a given market, where to invest within a particular market, and, most importantly, what type of property will yield the highest cash flow and ROI in that specific location.

Technology and software have democratized the short-term rental industry, eliminating the need for "insider knowledge" or reliance on a property management company to discern where or what type of property to invest in. While many software tools are available, I use AirDNA for most of my market research.

AirDNA utilizes a powerful combination of first-party data, comprehensive data scraped from sites like Airbnb and Vrbo, and partner data. This mix provides a rich and accurate market overview, simplifying complex analyses and displaying them on a user-friendly dashboard. I'll share a few very simple things that I look at on AirDNA that enable me to make smarter investment decisions and, ultimately, insane levels of cash flow with my properties. First of all, many of you are going to go to AirDNA's website and balk at the cost to access the information. Don't. If you are not leveraging data to make smarter investment decisions, you will ultimately pay far more for your mistakes with a property that does not cash flow. If you are not willing to invest in the necessary tools to make good investment decisions, you're going to invest tens of thousands—or hundreds of thousands—of dollars into a property blindly.

As I mentioned earlier, no market is perfect. But knowing which zip code to invest in, identifying where the top properties are, understanding how property size affects performance, and recognizing the amenities most attractive to travelers can lead to more profitable outcomes. The difference between a mediocre property and an excellent one in the right location, with the right design and amenities in the same market, can yield a difference of thousands of dollars per month in revenue and cash flow.

The very first thing I look at when logging on to AirDNA is not the daily rates, the occupancy tab, the revenue tab, or the splash page where AirDNA assigns a letter grade to that market. What I first look at is the active listings tab, filtering by revenue. Why? Because I can promise you that neither you nor I will be the first to invest in a given market. Have you ever heard the business adage that the first to market has the advantage, but the second to market earns all the money? It's not any different with short-term rentals. When filtering active listings by revenue, there are three specific aspects to focus on.

1. Observe on the map where the top properties are located. Are they all clustered in one or two areas of the town? Are they all in a single zip code or even within a specific neighborhood or street? If you notice clusters of top properties in certain areas, it's for a good reason. Location matters to travelers. If I find a specific pocket of a market where all the top performers are located, guess where I'm going to focus my efforts on searching for available properties? That same exact area!

2. Use filters to discern the difference in revenue potential among the top-performing properties. You can filter by zip code, number of bedrooms, property type, occupancy and more. Utilizing filters is crucial. If you see that the top four-bedroom properties in the entire market are generating over $200,000 per year in revenue, don't assume that acquiring any four-bedroom

property anywhere in that market will yield the same numbers. Applying the zip code filter will show you the top performers in each submarket. Adjusting filters based on the number of bedrooms or occupancy shows the variance in revenue potential based on property size. A higher revenue potential for four-bedroom properties in a specific zip code doesn't automatically mean they are a better investment than properties of another size in a different zip code. We also need to consider real estate costs and the differences between, for example, three- and four-bedroom properties, including the cost per square foot in zip code A versus zip code B. More details on this are provided in the next chapter when we delve into investment analysis.

3. Once we identify which zip codes or neighborhoods and property sizes yield the best results, I examine each of the top properties by clicking on their Airbnb or Vrbo listings. This is when I scroll through the photos and start taking notes. Observe what the top performers have in common. Do they all feature amenities like a hot tub, mountain views, a pool, large backyard, fire pit, or a home gym? Is the listing described as "walkable to Main Street"? You have all this information sitting in front of you; all you have to do is take notes and begin to identify trends.

After reviewing all the top properties, I take a look at the market performance details to observe the supply of active short-term rentals and how it has changed in recent years. Has the supply remained steady or increased significantly? Then, by looking at the revenue tab, you can track how revenue has fluctuated over the past several years. The total market revenue represents the combined income generated by all active rentals in that market. If the total supply has grown faster than the total market revenue, it's likely that the market as a whole could experience a decrease in RevPAR (Revenue Per Available Rental).

Just because supply has outpaced demand doesn't mean you can't make great cash flow in that market. It just means that competition is intensifying, and you need to be laser-focused. This underscores the importance of creating a property that competes with the top performers. As a short-term rental investor, our goal is to compete on value, not just price. Like in many industries, price competition is a race to the bottom. By competing on value and having superior design and amenities, you can achieve long-term success in a competitive market.

One key metric to understand is RevPAR. RevPAR is calculated by dividing the total market revenue by the total number of active rentals in that market, representing revenue per available rental, sometimes referred to as RevPAL or revenue per available listing. If RevPAR is declining year over year, it suggests that most rentals in that market will potentially experience diminishing returns, and short-term rental operators may have to compete more on price to secure bookings. You can find RevPAR data for a given market on AirDNA, and I encourage you to make note of trends in RevPAR over recent years.

I also encourage you to examine the occupancy and rates tabs on AirDNA. Notice the seasonality in occupancy: which months exhibit higher occupancy, and which months are lower? Has the occupancy rate increased, remained steady, or decreased over the past few years? On the rates tab, you'll observe that different types of properties—whether they're economy, mid-scale, upscale, or luxury—have varying historical daily rates. Additionally, by looking into the revenue tab, you can see the average revenue numbers for a given property type in a specific market for each month of recent years. For each of these tabs, I strongly recommend starting with a broad market overview and then diving into submarkets, using filters to weed out the data that isn't relevant based on the location, size, and type of property you're evaluating.

I suggest you look at the property earning potential (Rentalizer) section, but please approach this tool with caution as it is not infallible. The Rentalizer tab uses an algorithm to pull comparable listings and give you an estimated revenue potential based solely on the available data. I've found that, more often than not, the Rentalizer tool tends to underestimate the revenue a property can actually generate. Sometimes it is accurate, and rarely, it overestimates a property's potential. Keep in mind that the Rentalizer merely utilizes available information and an algorithm to generate such a forecast. It does not account for who is setting up the property, the improvements you plan to make, the amenities you intend to offer, or how you're ultimately going to market and manage the property.

Once you have a grasp of general market trends and the locations of top-performing properties, you should also conduct general market research. Start online to discover why people visit that specific market. What are the top attractions? What is the typical age of the traveler? What is the average group size traveling to that market? How long are they staying for? What other major developments are in the plans for that particular city in the coming years? Understanding these trends will help you narrow down your investment criteria and find winning properties more quickly.

With all this information at hand, it's time to create a "buy box." A buy box is simply defining the exact criteria of where to invest, what type of property you need to focus on, what design to implement, what amenities to provide, how many people to accommodate, how many bedrooms and bathrooms to have, and other specifics. The more precise your buy box criteria, the more of a sniper you become. Remember, the goal isn't to cast a wide net in hopes of landing a short-term rental cash cow. The goal is to be patient and know exactly what you're looking for and how to set it up for maximum success and cash flow.

Creating a buy box doesn't have to be a complicated process. It involves just a few key criteria. First, note where the top properties are located. Copy the Airbnb links for each of these properties and place them, hyperlinked, in a spreadsheet. Next to each property link, jot down the AirDNA revenue, the number of bedrooms and bathrooms, how many people the listing can accommodate, the zip code it's located in, and the type of amenities the property offers, such as a game room, hot tub, movie theater, etc. Do this for many properties, not just a few. You'll notice trends here. The properties with the highest revenue will be very similar in most cases.

Secondly, we need to compile a list of everything the top properties all have in common. If you're looking in the Smoky Mountains, for instance, you'd likely note a hot tub, game room, and mountain views. Write down which zip code(s) you will need to focus on. Note how many bedrooms and bathrooms your property needs and how many people it should accommodate. Replicating what others are doing will likely yield a similar result. But how do we take a similar property and make it perform in the top 1% of a market? We need to list our "over-the-top" amenities, which will help our property stand out from the current top performers. Let's say that very few (or zero) properties in a given market offer a movie theater or a golf simulator. Those are two amenities I would consider adding to achieve a higher nightly rate and occupancy than the competition. All of this gathered information formalizes your buy box.

Now that you have formalized your buy box and you're armed with all the necessary market information to hunt for a high cash-flowing short-term rental property, it's time to work with a local realtor who knows their stuff. Not all realtors are created equal. In fact, many realtors claim they understand short-term rentals, but most have no clue about the level of detail it takes to select a winning property. Just because someone has been a realtor for a decade in a market doesn't mean they understand how to invest in short-term rentals. Here's what I look for in a realtor.

They must be knowledgeable about the current short-term rental laws, regulations, and permit requirements. This is perhaps the most critical aspect of working with a realtor. The last thing you want is to be shown a bunch of properties that fit your buying criteria and then go under contract and close on one, only to find out that the city will not approve your short-term rental permit.

Do not make this mistake! Always verify yourself once a realtor suggests properties to ensure they are indeed short-term rental eligible. The realtor must have a finger on the pulse of the short-term rental industry in that specific market and understand which areas tend to rent better and why. They should work frequently with short-term rental investors, and it's a major bonus, though not a requirement, if they have short-term rental investments themselves.

Meeting these criteria will enable you to confidently provide your realtor with the buy box information you've compiled from your research. With this information, the realtor will know exactly where to look, what size property, and what features or amenities are required. Then, the realtor can start presenting you with available properties, both on and off-market, that are both short-term rental permit eligible and match your buy box criteria. Just because a property meets your buy box criteria doesn't always mean it's going to be a great investment. You need to subject these properties to a thorough and strict investment analysis to determine their viability. In the next chapter, we will dive deeper into how to analyze a deal and key investing metrics.

To recap, don't spend too much time trying to find the perfect market because it doesn't exist. Instead, conduct proper market research, define your buy box, and find a great opportunity within a sustainable market.

Leverage data available on sites like AirDNA to understand which ZIP codes and property types offer the highest revenue potential. Work with an experienced realtor who truly understands the local regulations and nuances of the given market.

CHAPTER FOUR

Key Investing Metrics and Investment Analysis

M any novice investors make one of two mistakes: they either blindly invest in a property with high expectations and scratch their heads when it doesn't perform well, or they pass up on great opportunities because they focus solely on one metric, such as the occupancy rate, instead of conducting a proper investment analysis. For example, don't just look at the average occupancy rate on AirDNA and assume that a 55% average occupancy rate for an entire market means the market is terrible and there are no good investment opportunities. Conversely, don't look at a market with an 80% occupancy rate and assume every property will be a home run. The occupancy rate is just one of many metrics we must consider. At the end of the day, the goal is to achieve the highest possible return on our investment. Always ask yourself: how hard is your money working for you?

Additionally, there are many other expenses to consider when acquiring and setting up a short-term rental compared to a long-term rental. It's critical to budget accordingly because the last thing you want is to purchase a property and then realize you don't have enough money to properly furnish it with the right design or amenities. The first part of our investment analysis involves calculating the total investment cost or the total amount of cash needed to acquire and set up our short-term rental property.

The first cost is the down payment, typically calculated as a percentage of the purchase price. The down payment requirement varies based on the type of loan, but for most investment loans, a 20% down payment is fairly standard. If your purchase price is $500,000 and you're putting down 20%, your down payment would be $100,000. If you plan to use the property for personal use as a vacation home, you might be able to put as little as 10% down. Speak with a loan officer to better understand your options based on your intentions with the property.

In addition to the down payment, we have to calculate our estimated closing costs. Closing costs associated with buying real estate include loan origination fees, appraisal fees, title fees and insurance, discount points, taxes, deed recording fees, and credit report charges. When buying a property, closing costs can vary based on your down payment, the type of loan, your credit score, and many other factors. Typically, I recommend budgeting anywhere from 4% to 7% of the purchase price for closing costs. It's wise to consult with a few loan officers to get an idea of the typical closing costs you can expect before going under contract based on the type of loan and purchase price. They should be able to give you a more accurate estimate based on current economic conditions.

If the property isn't turnkey—meaning it's not ready to rent as soon as you close—then you may have to cover costs such as new paint, replacing old carpet, landscaping, etc. If you're undertaking a more extensive rehab, you might need to completely remodel the kitchen, bathrooms, or even convert a garage into another bedroom, for example. It's important to account for these costs in the investment details section. If you're a new investor, rehab costs can be tricky to estimate. I recommend conducting thorough research online to understand the costs of various tasks (like painting a house) in the specific market you're considering and also calling a few general contractors for rough quotes ahead of time if possible. Then, add an extra 10-20% on top of your estimated costs. Rehab costs in real estate tend to exceed budgets more often than not. Trust me—I've underestimated rehab costs more times than I'd like to admit.

Since we're setting up a short-term rental, we must also consider the cost of professional design, setup, and staging the property. If you're outsourcing design to a company such as Somerled Designs, you'll need to include their design fee here, in addition to the cost of the furniture alone. If you're not the one setting up the furniture and staging the property, I recommend adding a line item for local contractor labor. Websites like Taskrabbit can connect you with people who can help assemble furniture and perform other tasks to set up your rental efficiently. Of course, you can choose to design and set everything up yourself. I did this for my first six properties, and while we saved some money doing it ourselves, I'll be the first to tell you that this is the most challenging, time-consuming, and stressful part of the entire process. Since then, I have had Somerled Designs handle the design of all my properties and outsourced the rehab, unboxing, furnishing, and staging to local contractors. Our newer properties that were professionally designed and set up perform significantly better than the ones we did on our own.

Next, we need to calculate the amount we expect to spend on furniture. This can vary depending on the size of the house, the total usable square footage, the number of bedrooms, and common and outdoor spaces. As a general rule of thumb, I typically budget (at a minimum) $5,000–7,500 per room or space. For instance, if a property has four bedrooms, one living room, and a large outdoor patio, I would multiply six total spaces by $5,000 for a smaller property or multiply six by $7,500 for a larger or more upscale property. So, in this scenario, I would expect to spend between $30,000 and $45,000 on furniture, decor, and amenities. Yes, I know that may come as a shock, but proper design, furniture, and amenities will absolutely yield higher revenue, cash flow, and return on your investment. If this property had a larger square footage or I was outfitting it with more expensive amenities, I would lean towards the higher estimate of $45,000 for furniture. Similar to rehab costs, I prefer to err on the side of caution when estimating my expenses, as they can quickly add up. (Further details on actually budgeting for every line item of furniture are provided later on.)

Lastly, we need to consider any other costs associated with setting up our property. Are there any business licenses you need to apply for and pay locally? Will you be driving a long distance to and from your property every day for several weeks while setting it up? Do you have to pay for any short-term rental or fire department inspections before launching? These costs are not typically high, but it's important to account for each and every cost associated with setting up a property and keep track of them all.

Once you have all these items, we can add them up. That would include the total down payment, estimated closing costs, rehab, design, furniture, and setup costs, which will give us the total amount of cash we expect to invest. The next step in our investment analysis is to better understand how to create a forecast for our annual and average monthly rental income.

First, let's walk through some key metrics that you'll need to familiarize yourself with when it comes to short-term rental investing.

- First is the average daily rate (ADR). This is the average daily price at which you can expect your property to be booked throughout a given year.

- Second is the occupancy rate. Unlike long-term rental investors, we don't use the vacancy rate to estimate how many days per year our unit will be left vacant. Instead, we use the occupancy rate, or the total number of days we expect to be rented out throughout a given year, divided by 365 days. For example, if you expect to be rented out 225 nights per year, to calculate your occupancy rate, you would simply divide 225 by 365, which would yield a 61.64% occupancy rate.

In order to calculate our forecasted revenue, we simply take our ADR and multiply it by the number of days we expect to be booked throughout the year. For instance, if we have an expected ADR of $300 and an occupancy rate of 61.64%, as mentioned earlier, we would multiply $300 by 225 days, resulting in a forecasted revenue of $67,500, or $5,625 per month. Creating an accurate forecast for a short-term rental is significantly more challenging than for a long-term rental property. Both daily rates and occupancy rates can fluctuate not just annually or monthly, as with long-term rentals, but on a daily basis. The difference between a mediocre short-term rental managed poorly and an excellent one managed effectively can amount to thousands of dollars per month. This is why understanding these metrics and forecasting accurately is so important.

It's great to forecast a high revenue, but our ultimate goal is positive cash flow. A short-term rental could be generating $10,000 per month, but if total expenses exceed $10,000 per month, then you're actually losing money each month in terms of cash flow. Remember, generating sufficient cash flow to cover your living expenses is what's going to set you financially free! Next, let's explore the typical monthly operating expenses we can expect to incur and calculate our net operating income.

First, we have property taxes and insurance. While these are often included in a mortgage payment, they're technically operating expenses and not part of the actual debt service, which covers principal and interest. We need to consider fees such as HOA fees, if applicable, and utilities like water, gas, electricity, Wi-Fi, and cable/streaming services, if provided. We also need to budget for future capital expenditures (CAPEX), like replacing the HVAC system or roof. While we rarely need to spend money on these types of capital expenditures on a month-to-month basis, we do need to account for them in our analysis. Additionally, we need to budget for incidentals like soap, coffee, toilet paper, other paper products, cleaning supplies, and anything else we'd like to provide for guests. We need to budget for general maintenance costs, which may include pest control, landscaping, pool maintenance, and general repairs such as plumbing or electrical work. Whatever you estimate for general maintenance, I'd recommend adding an extra 25% to the cost, as there is always a random expense that pops up from time to time.

We also have to budget for any software tools that we plan to use. These would be things such as your property management software, dynamic pricing, and turnover (cleaning) management. These tools are relatively inexpensive, but altogether, I'd recommend budgeting $75–$100 per month for the general tech stack. If your city requires an annual short-term rental permit, remember to include this fee here as well. Since permits are typically paid annually, make sure to adjust the number in monthly operating expenses and divide it by 12 here.

For example, if your annual permit expense is $300, divide this by 12 to forecast a monthly expense of $25 for permitting fees. If you're not self-managing, you should also include the property management fee if outsourcing to a property management company like Home Team Vacation Rentals. I prefer to display this as a percentage of expected revenue in our forecast and calculate it as a monthly expense as well). Most property management companies charge between 15% on the low end and as high as 35% in some markets. To accurately forecast this expense, it's crucial to understand the typical property management fee in your target market if you plan to outsource management. If your forecasted revenue is $10,000 per month, and your property management fee is 20%, you should account for $2,000 per month in your monthly expenses for property management. Additionally, you need to budget for service fees for using platforms such as Airbnb or Vrbo. Double-check what Airbnb and Vrbo are currently charging hosts and ensure you budget accordingly. At the time of writing this book, I typically budget 3% of revenue for this line item. All these factors contribute to your total monthly operating expenses.

One aspect to note here is cleaning fees. I didn't mention cleaning fees because, when analyzing short-term rental properties, I don't include cleaning fees in my revenue forecast or as an operating expense. However, as of writing this book, it's important to note that AirDNA's historical data includes cleaning fees in both the average daily rates and the revenue projections it shows for any given property. If you're using AirDNA's Rentalizer to craft your forecast, ensure you're including cleaning fees in both your operating expenses and revenue! The reason I prefer to exclude cleaning fee revenue and expenses is that it's impossible to accurately predict the exact number of cleans you'll have throughout a year or even in a given month.

For instance, you could have two renters staying for 15 days each, filling the entire month, or you could have ten different renters with numerous short stays within the same month. In one scenario, you have two cleans, and in the other, you have 10. If your cleaning fee is $100, you're looking at either $200 or $1,000 in cleaning fees—a big difference! The way I look at it is that if you are charging guests $100 or more for a cleaning fee and paying your cleaners $100 per clean, it's a wash. That said, to create a more accurate forecast of actual cash flow, cash-on-cash return, and total ROI, I prefer to exclude cleaning fees from the calculation. It's worth noting that when you realize revenue on an active rental, you will capture the cleaning fees you charge to guests as rental income, and cleaning fees will more than likely be your highest monthly expenses.

However, stripping cleaning fees out of both revenue and operating expenses in your forecast should make your realized cash flow align more closely with your initial analysis. Some people will argue that this is a bad way to do it. For me, it makes forecasting easier and more accurate.

To calculate net operating income (NOI), you simply subtract your operating expenses from your forecasted revenue. Although capitalization rates (cap rates) don't have much, if any, effect on how a single-family home is appraised in value today, it is a good thing to calculate and compare your property's cap rate to the local market average to gauge the strength of your investment relative to other real estate investment opportunities. Cap rate is determined by dividing a property's NOI by its current market value. For instance, if your NOI is $50,000 per year and the property's current value is $500,000, your investment has a 10% cap rate. Why is this important? Cap rate is crucial because it strips the debt service out of the equation and simply looks at how strong the investment is compared to other real estate opportunities in the market. Single-family homes are appraised based on recently sold comparable properties in the market, not on net operating income and cap rate, like commercial real estate is. Therefore, increasing the operating income of a single-family home doesn't directly enhance its appraisal value through forced appreciation.

Conversely, if a commercial property had an NOI of $50,000 with a local cap rate of 10%, its value would be calculated as $50,000 divided by 0.1 (or 10%), resulting in an appraised value of $500,000. If you were to buy a commercial property and increase the operating income to $60,000, and the local cap rate was 10%, you would effectively force appreciation on the property, and it would now be valued at $600,000. But enough on cap rates since you likely won't be basing your investment decisions for single-family short-term rental properties on it. Let's move on to calculate cash flow and, most importantly, cash-on-cash return.

To calculate your monthly cash flow, subtract the debt service (the principal and interest portion of your mortgage) from the expected monthly NOI. It may seem counterintuitive, but just because a property has a high cash flow doesn't necessarily mean it is automatically a good investment! And conversely, a lower cash flow doesn't necessarily mean it's a bad investment. Why is this the case?

As real estate investors, we have to have a keen understanding of how hard our money is working for us. My primary focus during an investment analysis is the cash-on-cash return (COC return). COC return measures the annual cash flow divided by the total all-in cost of the investment, expressed as a percentage. The higher the COC return, the stronger the investment's performance from a cash flow perspective. For example, if your forecasted annual cash flow is $30,000 and the total cash invested is $120,000, to calculate COC return, you'd simply divide $30,000 by $120,000, yielding a 25% COC return. This is the number one metric most real estate investors use to judge the health and performance of their investments.

Historically, most long-term rental investors have aimed for an 8%–10% COC return. In a high-interest-rate environment, many long-term rental investors might not anticipate any positive COC return in the first year or two in business, as they only expect to cash flow down the road when rents increase in their market, or they're able to refinance to a lower interest rate. Since short-term rentals offer a higher potential for cash flow and require more effort and work to set up and manage, I typically target an 18%–20% COC return for all my short-term rental investments that I self-manage, with an upside target of 30% or higher COC return if we hit our high-side forecast. If you outsource the property management, I would expect the COC return to be lower, around 10%–15%. The COC return will largely be dictated by the type of loan used and the down payment amount (more details on this later). While COC return is an excellent indicator of how well the investment is performing from a cash flow perspective, it does not tell us the whole story. After all, when it comes to investing in real estate, cash flow is what sets you financially free, but the equity, appreciation, and tax benefits will build your wealth long-term.

In addition to cash-on-cash return, I suggest looking at the total return on investment (total ROI) for a more holistic view of your real estate investments over the long term rather than focusing solely on cash flow. To calculate total ROI, you first need to sum up the total expected annual cash flow, the first 12 months of principal paydown on the mortgage, any expected property appreciation (historically around 4% YoY in the U.S.), and any forced appreciation if you spent money to rehab the property and increased the value of it. Then, divide that total by the amount of cash invested in the property to get your total ROI. For example, let's say your subject property is expected to generate $30,000 in annual cash flow, with a first-year principal paydown of $10,000, no significant rehab for forced appreciation, and an expected 4% property appreciation on a $500,000 property value, equating to a $20,000 increase in property value.

To calculate total ROI, we simply add up our expected cash flow ($30,000), principal paydown ($10,000), and appreciation ($20,000) to get $60,000. If the total cash invested into this property was $120,000, our total ROI would be calculated by dividing $60,000 by $120,000, giving us a 50% total ROI. Once you start finding good deals, this will be an eye-popping number and make you question why you would ever want to invest in other asset classes, such as the stock market, mutual funds, or traditional long-term rentals. The reason I like looking at a total ROI and not just COC return is that it gives me a true understanding of what the expected return on my money invested actually is, not just the cash flow.

One additional metric I want to discuss is return on equity (ROE). This was a key takeaway for me from *The Millionaire Real Estate Investor* by Gary Keller. An interesting aspect to note is that your COC return typically increases over time. Since your revenue tends to increase more than your expenses do each year, your cash flow will increase each year, which leads to a YoY increase in the annual COC return. This is a good thing!

Your equity position will also increase over time. Remember, we have a principal paydown on the mortgage and home appreciation, which compounds over time. ROE is calculated by taking your total annual cash flow and dividing it by the total equity position you currently have in that property. For example, let's assume you have a $500,000 property and your equity position is $100,000 at the end of year one. If that property cash flowed you $20,000 that year, you had a 20% return on equity ($20,000 divided by $100,000). Let's assume that in five years, that property will be worth $600,000, for a total of $200,000 in equity. Your equity position is now the original $100,000 plus an additional $100,000 from appreciation. (In reality, you'd have more equity, including principal paydown, but for the sake of this example, we will just look at appreciation.)

This is the beauty of leverage in real estate. Although you borrowed 80% of the money to buy that property, you keep 100% of the appreciation. Now, during those five years, your cash flow has likely increased somewhat year over year as well. Let's assume your cash flow is now $25,000 per year. To calculate your new ROE at the end of year five, we would take the $25,000 cash flow and divide it by $200,000 of equity, which yields us a 12.5% ROE. In just five years, your cash flow went up, and cash-on-cash return also increased, while your ROE was almost cut in half. Crazy, right? If you have ever wondered why a lot of real estate investors never buy their properties with cash, and many of them do cash-out refinances or 1031 exchanges to acquire more properties, it is because they want to maximize their ROE.

By doing a cash-out refinance or a 1031 exchange, you can repurpose some or all of the equity in a property you own into more or larger real estate investments, which will ultimately yield a higher overall ROE, and you can defer paying taxes on those gains while doing so. When you do a refinance or a 1031 exchange, you postpone capital gains taxes until a sale occurs and a capital gain is realized. Leveraging equity in current real estate investments helps real estate investors scale faster in most cases. As you grow as a real estate investor, pay attention to the ROE for each of your investments!

As you become proficient at evaluating properties, you will notice how significantly even small changes can influence your cash flow, and COC return in average daily rate and occupancy rate can swing.

When forecasting an average daily rate and occupancy, always start with available data on sites such as AirDNA to establish a baseline, and then narrow down the data to get as granular as possible. In order to craft the most accurate forecast and investment analysis possible, you must sharpen the forecast by looking directly at active short-term rental comps in the same area as your subject property. I recommend identifying the top three to five comps that are in a similar area to your property. This is not just the same market! I recommend you look in the same zip code and, often, in the same neighborhood if possible. You'll need to look for properties that have the same number of bedrooms, accommodate around the same number of people, have similar amenities, comparable design, etc. This is critical. I have many new students in BNB Investor Academy who come to me to review a deal, excited, claiming they found a property with a 50% COC return. When we dive into the data, we find that there are properties producing the level of revenue they are forecasting, but they are not in the same zip code and have additional amenities that cannot be installed in this property, such as a pool or theater room.

You have to filter out all the irrelevant data in order to create a hyper-accurate forecast. For example, if you have a four-bedroom property and you're looking for four-bedroom comps in South Florida, but yours does not have a pool, ensure you are not comparing it to properties with pools because you will not rent for the same amount per night, nor as frequently in many cases. Once you narrow down your top three to five comps, look at their listings directly on Airbnb. Check their reviews to ensure they have numerous recent reviews. If they only have three reviews from a year ago and none since it is not a valid comp. If the property has only been active for a short period of time (one to two months), it may not be a good comp. If the property has 50 reviews but hasn't had a review in over six months, it likely doesn't provide reliable data either. Examine their calendars to see exactly what they are charging on any given day of the week and any given month throughout the year. Observe their charges on weekends, weekdays, holidays, and different months or seasons. Note their future bookings and how far in advance they are getting booked. All of these data points matter! The more accurate the data, the better the comp is.

Once you compile a list of good comps, it should give you more confidence in your forecast and a higher conviction to either proceed with the investment or not. The last thing you want is to over-forecast and be surprised by less rental income, less cash flow, and a lower COC return. You also don't want to pass up a good investment opportunity because you under-forecasted!

Once you have crafted what we believe to be an accurate forecast and COC return, you should stress test the investment analysis. By this, I mean examine both the downside and the upside of the investment. Remember, there are some things outside of our control, and we want to make sure we understand not just the upside of an investment but also the downside. Let's assume that you're forecasting a $300 average daily rate and a 65% occupancy. What if you fall short of this forecast and ultimately end up renting at $250 a night and only achieve a 60% occupancy? How does this affect your cash flow and your COC return? I typically aim for my downside forecast to be somewhere between a 7%–10% COC return, which would match the historical returns of the stock market.

I also want to know what the upside is. After all, if you execute on your vision and have great design, proper amenities, implement a good pricing strategy, and manage effectively, you will have an opportunity to outperform your baseline forecast. What does the upside look like in this case? Are the top properties renting for $350 a night and have a 70% occupancy? I typically look for the upside in my investments to be a 30% COC return or higher. Indeed, with short-term rentals, it's possible to achieve a far higher return than that. In fact, I have hit a 100% cash-on-cash return on a property I purchased in the past. Is it rare? Yes. Is it still possible? Absolutely!

Stress testing the investment analysis should give us a higher level of conviction in our investment decisions. I tend to be a bit conservative with my forecast and overall investment analysis because, at the end of the day, I would rather be pleasantly surprised by slightly more cash flow and a higher COC return than less.

Performing an effective analysis doesn't have to be difficult. Grab a free copy of my personal investment analysis template. Scan the QR code here.

CHAPTER FIVE

Understanding Loans and Financing Options

W hen it comes to purchasing short-term rentals, there are various financing options available. The most common type of loan for a single-family home is a conventional loan. A conventional loan is a type of mortgage loan that is not backed by a government agency. Conventional loans are divided into two general categories: conforming and non-conforming loans. A conforming loan simply means that the loan adheres to the guidelines established by the Federal National Mortgage Association (Fannie Mae) and the Federal Home Loan Mortgage Corporation (Freddie Mac). These two government-backed mortgage companies buy mortgages from lenders and either hold these mortgages in their portfolios or package the loans into what is known as mortgage-backed securities (MBS), which are ultimately sold on the secondary market.

Conforming loans have limits set by the Federal Housing Finance Agency (FHFA) each year, which often increase year over year. There is a base limit that most geographical areas fall under; however, certain areas, such as New York City or San Francisco, have much higher limits since housing is far more expensive in these cities. In 2023, for example, the conforming loan limit for most areas in the United States was $726,200, and in 2024 it increased to $766,550. Remember, this is the loan limit, not the purchase price. If you were putting 20% down on a property and wanted to stay within the conforming loan limit, your maximum purchase price in 2024 would be $958,187.50 ($766,550 divided by 0.8).

A nonconforming loan is simply a loan that does not conform to the purchasing guidelines set forth by Fannie Mae and Freddie Mac, or which is larger than the conforming loan limit for the given location. Just because a loan is larger than the conforming limit doesn't mean you cannot find a loan for the property. This means that the loan will be considered a nonconforming jumbo loan and will have different eligibility requirements. Often, you will need a higher credit score and a lower debt-to-income ratio (DTI) to qualify for a jumbo loan. Other types of nonconforming loans are those that are insured by the federal government, making them less risky for lenders and providing more affordable options for buyers. The three main types of government-backed loans are FHA loans, VA loans, and USDA loans. Each of these types of loans comes with different down payment and credit score criteria. Many of these loans require that you occupy the property as your primary residence.

When buying a short-term rental, most people start out by leveraging a conforming second home loan or an investment loan. If you're using a second home loan, your intent cannot be purely for investment purposes. A second home loan is meant for those with the intent to buy a vacation home for their own use or for their family. However, you are allowed to rent out the vacation home when you are not personally using it. Keep in mind that if you rent the property for more than 14 days per year, you will be responsible for reporting and paying taxes on the rental income. Second home loans should not be used to buy real estate that is being purchased solely for investment purposes. The advantage of buying a vacation home and renting it out when you are not using it is that the minimum down payment requirement is just 10%, and, of course, you can likely have a vacation home paid for by people renting it out, rather than it sitting vacant between your visits. With a second home loan, you have to qualify for the loan yourself, and you cannot use any projected rental income to help you qualify.

I caution you never to utilize a second home loan if your sole intent is to purchase an investment property, as this would be considered occupancy or mortgage fraud. If the sole intent is to purchase the property for investment purposes, I'd recommend you use an investment loan.

For conforming investment loans, the minimum down payment (at the time of writing this book) is 15% for qualified buyers. The benefit of using an investment loan is that lenders may use up to 75% of the projected rental income to offset the mortgage payment for an investment property purchase. (Projected rental income is typically based on projections as a long-term rental, not a short-term rental.)

This can help you get a mortgage for an investment property for which you may not qualify based solely on your current income and DTI.

While leveraging conventional financing is great, it does have its limits. According to Fannie Mae, any one individual can have a maximum of ten conventional loans in their name at a given time. So, eventually, you will either max out on the number of conventional loans you can have, or you'll reach a limit on your debt-to-income ratio (DTI) and will struggle to qualify for more conventional loans. At this point, you will likely have to pivot to additional financing options.

If so, you will likely consider commercial lending options and loans that use the debt service coverage ratio (DSCR) to qualify you for the mortgage instead of your own DTI. With DSCR, lenders focus on the projected rental income of a subject property rather than your individual ability to service the debt. Most lenders refer to an income-based appraisal report to justify a fair estimated monthly rental income that a subject property could generate. Typically, lenders will use 75% of the 12-month average rental income as a long-term rental in the DSCR approach.

Although this metric varies, most lenders look for a minimum debt service coverage ratio of 1:1 or higher, meaning that 75% of the monthly projected rental income needs to be the same amount or higher than the monthly mortgage payment. Lenders may have different requirements for DSCR-type loans, so make sure to inquire with different lenders or loan officers to see which option is best suited for your investment.

Alternatively, if no actual rent is available as a long-term rental, many lenders are now making short-term rental exceptions for properties intended to be rented as a short-term rental. Some lenders will consider the AirDNA Rentalizer value that may be used at the underwriter's discretion or a rental income projection provided by a professional property management company for the subject property. As time goes on and more data becomes available and normalized in the lending industry, I'd imagine lenders will use more creative ways to justify the rental income projections on short-term rental properties to qualify based on DSCR.

Keep in mind that loans using the DSCR approach often come with less favorable terms. They typically feature higher closing costs, higher interest rates, and often stiff prepayment penalties. Because commercial loans are intended to be between a financial institution and a business, you will more than likely be required to close in a business name and not in your personal name. This means you will need to close in an LLC.

Lastly, I want to caution you that lending requirements change frequently, and some of the information in this chapter may no longer be relevant depending on when you are reading this book. I suggest working with an experienced loan officer who works with many investors to figure out what the best lending options are for you based on your current circumstances and goals. They will also stay up to date on the different types of loans and the requirements for each.

One thing I want to touch on is insurance for your short-term rental. Insurance for short-term rentals is going to be more complicated than ordinary homeowners' insurance. You should start evaluating insurance providers while you are under contract, and you'll need to select a policy to bind coverage before you close. As a short-term rental owner, you need commercial liability insurance. At the end of the day, you are running a business and need to be insured as such. You'll want a policy that covers the building, contents, loss of rental income, $1,000,000–$2,000,000 in general liability insurance, and more.

There are only a few companies out there, such as Proper Insurance, that provide commercial liability insurance for short-term rentals at the time of writing this book. As time goes on, I'm sure there will be more providers that bring new, effective policies to market. I'll say this one last time: Please ensure that you have the appropriate insurance coverage for your short-term rental property! Yes, premiums are going to be more expensive, but it is necessary.

For example, someone I previously worked with was insured by Proper Insurance and had adequate coverage. The following year, the insurance premium went up and she canceled the policy for a cheaper alternative that did not provide adequate coverage to include things such as loss of rental income. One day, while her cleaners were turning the unit, a lighted sign on the wall caused a fire to start, which burned down the house. Sadly, their insurance provider did not cover the loss of rental income while the rental property was left vacant, and they figured out the next steps. It is critical that you have adequate insurance to operate your business.

One of the most common questions I get from new investors is whether they need an LLC (limited liability company). The short answer is: Yes! Whether you buy the property and close in an LLC, however, is a different answer. If you are closing with a conventional loan, you will not be able to close in an LLC. However, if you are using a commercial loan, you will more than likely be required to close in an LLC. There are ways to move the property into an LLC after closing, but be aware of something called a due-on-sale clause. This is a clause most mortgage providers use that allows them to call the remainder of the loan "due on sale," meaning if you sell or transfer the property, they have the right to call the loan due. This happens very rarely when transferring the deed over to your LLC, but it is possible.

Some states have a high transfer tax. If they charge a 2% transfer tax and you move the title of your property from your name to your LLC, you will have a tax bill equal to 2% of the value of your property! If you owned a $1,000,000 property and had a 2% transfer tax, you'd end up paying $20,000! There are some creative ways around this, such as using land trusts. I would advise you to consult with a licensed attorney to ensure you are setting up your business and asset protection structure correctly.

LLCs are for asset protection. As your business and assets grow, it's important to properly segment and protect your assets. There is a lot of nuance to the proper way to structure your LLCs, but I will tell you, first and foremost, to work with a licensed attorney whose primary business is real estate. It's also a huge bonus if they have a focus on short-term rental investors as a client base. Each state has different laws and taxes associated with real estate ownership, title transfers, etc. I am not an attorney, nor do I have the time to figure all this stuff out on my own, which is why I personally outsource it to a pro. And I recommend you do the same.

CHAPTER SIX

How to Design, Furnish & Stage Your Property Like a Pro

O nce you have selected a property to invest in, the two most important determining factors for your property to compete at a high level are design and amenities. These will be two of the largest deciding factors in both how much cash flow you make and what helps you compete long-term in a competitive market and avoid diminishing returns.

Why is design so important? Well, think about it from the traveler's perspective. In order for a traveler to book your property, they first have to see your listing appear in search results on sites such as Airbnb or Vrbo; and second, they have to be intrigued enough to click on your listing and want to learn more about it. Our attention spans as humans have shrunk over time, largely due to the rapid growth and consumption of social media and short-form content. I view online travel agencies (OTAs), such as Airbnb, no differently than scrolling on Instagram or TikTok. On social media, you're scrolling through hundreds, if not thousands, of different photos or videos, waiting till one catches your attention, and then you pause. You wait a few seconds and decide if that piece of content is worth consuming in its entirety. You typically have about two seconds to grab someone's attention online, to make them stop and want to learn more.

A traveler has hundreds, if not thousands, of properties to scroll through in a given market. You first need to earn a click, after which the traveler will land on your listing splash page and have access to just five photos and your listing description. From there, they will decide if it's worth their time to click "see all photos" and scroll through the rest of the listing to assess whether it's worth booking. If your design and amenities do not stand out from the other properties travelers are considering, they will book somewhere else every time. The only exception will be if you are competing solely on price and are cheaper than everyone else, and the traveler is simply looking for the cheapest accommodation.

Having better design and amenities will enable you to secure bookings at a higher daily rate during the busy season and help you get booked, while others do not, during the slow season. It will increase your success as a short-term rental, and ensure that you make more over time without encountering diminishing returns like many average properties do. Think about it from a traveler's perspective. You have multiple listings in front of you in the same neighborhood, all with a similar floor plan and accommodate the same number of guests. If one of those listings features incredible design, professional photos, and more amenities, you're more likely to not only book the listing but also book it at a higher rate. This will keep your listing relevant in the long term as well. As many markets get more competitive, it is important to compete on value and experience rather than price. Competing on price is a race to the bottom and is a loser's game. I want to own properties people are willing to pay more for because they really want to stay there, not ones they select because it is the cheapest possible accommodation.

You now understand how critical design is, but where do you even begin? The initial research phase begins when you are evaluating a market on AirDNA. Look at top-performing properties and craft your buy box criteria. You should already know what the top amenities are and what types of design top-performing properties have in common. Make sure you write down a list of non-negotiable amenities and over-the-top amenities in your buy box! You should have links to the top properties saved so you can reference them easily.

Once you have a property under contract or a lease signed, if you are doing rental arbitrage, it's time to start getting organized and begin furnishing the entire property on a spreadsheet before ordering a single item to ensure you are within your budget. If you are going to be doing the design and furniture selection on your own, I recommend using websites such as Pinterest to get inspiration and building your own mood boards to finalize the overall theme you are going for. Piecing together a vision will make selecting furniture, paint colors, wallpaper, and everything else much easier.

Before you begin selecting any furniture, you need to get measurements of each space in the property. The last thing you want is to have a couch that is too small for the living room or order a king bed that doesn't fit in a bedroom. There are two options here. The first is a Matterport scan. This will scan your entire property and essentially build a virtual model of it, along with the dimensions of each room. If you are unable to do a Matterport scan, you will have to rely either on a floor plan of the property (if you can get your hands on one) or go and take measurements yourself to create a floor plan. Of these options, I strongly recommend ordering a Matterport scan. It is relatively inexpensive and will save you a ton of time. Once you have the dimensions and floor plan, you can begin your search to select furniture.

I recommend using a simple spreadsheet. After all, it is important to stay organized, considering you will be ordering dozens, if not hundreds, of different items for your property. In the spreadsheet, label different tabs for different sections of the property, for example, kitchen, living, dining, bedrooms, bathrooms, etc. Within each section, you need to start placing links to every single item of furniture or decor that you plan to purchase. Next to the item name and link, put the cost of that item and then the quantity you need to order. Then you can multiply the quantity of each item by the unit cost to get the total. Once you have all your items selected, you can add up the total amount for each dedicated space and ultimately add up the spaces to get the total amount you can expect to pay for furnishing the property.

This is helpful because, at the end of the day, this is an investment, and you need to budget accordingly. Sometimes, you complete the furniture budget analysis and realize that you are way over budget, and you'll have to figure out which areas or items to cut back on. Or you may be under budget and realize that you can allocate some of that surplus to adding more amenities that may boost your property's performance.

If you're unfamiliar with how to properly design a short-term rental, I strongly recommend considering working with a company such as Somerled Designs, which specializes in designing vacation rentals to help owners maximize their cash flow and their return on investment.

There are a few reasons I outsource the design on all my properties nowadays.

First, design and furniture selection is the most stressful and time-consuming part for most investors, including myself. It's not something I excel at, and I find my time is better spent on other activities within my businesses.

Second, I simply do a subpar job compared to the professional designers at Somerled Designs, and the difference between great design and mediocre design can amount to thousands of dollars in cash flow every year.

Third, speed to market is crucial. Every day your property isn't listed for rent represents an opportunity cost equal to your expected average daily rate. Getting your property live quickly, without cutting corners, can save you a significant amount in opportunity costs.

Somerled Designs offers two different packages: remote design or full turnkey design. With remote design, they will design the entire property for you and select every item of furniture. They then do a design handoff and provide instructions on how to order everything and set up the property. You will then procure the furniture and set everything up. For their full in-person design service, they handle everything for you, from designing the property, working with local contractors, doing the full install of design and furniture in person, and even staging and photographing the property for you.

To see more of Somerled Design's work and to inquire about their services, scan the QR code, visit www.somerleddesigns.com or follow @somerled.designs on social media.

By outsourcing one of the most time-consuming and stressful aspects of setting up a short-term rental, you can list the property for rent more quickly. In addition to design, outsourcing any labor, such as painting, assembling furniture, staging the property, etc., can often allow you to launch your property days earlier, if not weeks.

Once you have all your furniture selected and you are within your budget, I recommend starting to order furniture as soon as you close on the property or your lease begins. The only time I would wait to order furniture is if I was performing a larger rehab on the property and had nowhere to store the furniture. In that case, waiting to order most items makes sense. Make sure to check the shipping lead times on all the furniture. The last thing you want is to be waiting eight weeks for a couch when the rest of the items are delivered within the first three weeks. If that's the case, simply find another couch. Most items are not worth delaying the launch of your property and costing you a large sum of money in opportunity and holding costs.

As you order items, keep track of what has been ordered in your spreadsheet. The easiest way to do this is by highlighting the line items in a different color as soon as they are ordered. Once they are delivered, go back to the same spreadsheet and highlight them in another color to signify this status. Organization is critical! What you want to avoid is to have most of the house furnished and photos scheduled, only to realize that one or two items never showed up or were lost in transit, and you didn't realize through all the chaos of setting up your property that items were missing. This is why noting what has been delivered is important.

Once you have all your furniture delivered and set up, it's time to schedule your deep clean and stage your property for photos. I'll say this one time for you:

Do not take photos with your phone, and do not get photos done by a run-of-the-mill photographer who is not familiar with real estate photography specific to short-term rentals.

Average photos and poor editing will cost you thousands of dollars in opportunity costs. You will end up ranking lower in OTA search results, which can have a monumental impact on your listing performance. Remember, in order to get booked, you first have to show up in search results, get clicked on, and earn someone's attention!

I suggest having photos taken both during the daytime and at twilight (sunset shots), especially if you have any outdoor spaces that you want to highlight on your listing. Twilight photos are moody and can really help your listing stand out. Remember, you are marketing and selling an experience, not just a property. It is critical to stage the home properly to make the most of your photos. You want your photos staged so that it feels like the traveler can jump through the screen and see themselves having a great time at the property before they even make a reservation.

Set the dining table. Stage some drinks or juice on the table, along with a meat and cheese board. Drape throw blankets over the back of a sofa or chairs in the house. If you have a pool, throw in some large, colorful pool floats, such as a flamingo. If you have a hot tub, make sure the cover is off and the lights are on. If you have lounge chairs by the pool, place rolled-up pool towels at the end of the lounge chairs and maybe stage a few magazines or sunglasses for some detailed shots. Have a fire pit? Ensure there's a fire burning in it, or get the photographer to edit a fire into the shot. Outdoor lighting, such as string lights? Make sure they are on, especially for twilight photos. All of your TVs in the house need to have something edited on the screen to make it look like they are on, such as a movie scene or sports game. If you have any outdoor games, stage them in the yard. If you want to get really creative, depending on what type of traveler avatar you are catering towards, staging models in some of the photos can help.

Some of the best listings that cater to bachelorette parties, for example, have models staged in photos by the pool or in front of murals within the property. It helps travelers see themselves there, immersed in the experience before even booking. The list goes on, but you get the point. Trust me: if you don't stage your property well, your listing will suffer. If you need some inspiration, go look at some of the top-performing properties in your market and see how the property is staged in the photos.

You will notice the difference in how you feel while viewing great photos in a thoughtfully designed and staged property.

When designing a property, you'll want to consider what your particular wow factor will be. What is your unique selling proposition? What is the one thing you can provide that very few or no other properties provide in that market? Remember the "buy box" we talked about earlier? You need to know what your wow factor is before ever buying the property in the first place. The most compelling aspect of your property will likely be the subject of your first photo on your listing. This is what will trigger people to stop in their tracks and immediately think to themselves, *This looks really cool, I want to click and learn more about this property.* People want to book short-term rentals that provide the best possible experience that fits their budget. Give them a reason to stretch their budget to book your property. This can be one specific amenity or an "Instagrammable" moment, such as an interactive mural. People will pay extra for the opportunity to create a special memory they can't get anywhere else. Don't underestimate the importance of your "wow" factor.

People love creating memories while on vacation, especially if it's for a special occasion such as a bachelorette party or a once-a-year family reunion. If they post on social media, it's free marketing for you and your property. Many novice short-term rental investors look at going as cheaply as possible on their property to save money. You need to shift from a money-saving mindset to a money-making mindset. It is worth investing the extra money if—and only if—it helps increase your return on investment. If you are stuck on a decision to invest in a particular amenity or putting more into design, take the guesswork out of it and run the numbers. Conduct a side-by-side comparison of the investment analysis. Create one scenario where you're not investing extra money and another where you are. In the scenario where you're investing more, make sure to adjust your daily rate and occupancy accordingly based on the data you gather from researching comparable properties. Compare the two scenarios' cash-on-cash (COC) return. If the COC return goes up, invest the extra money. If it goes down, it might not be worth it. If your COC return stays the same, I'd encourage you to invest the extra money. Why? Because it's not only about the first year's cash-on-cash return but also about future years. You'll want to avoid diminishing returns and ensure longevity in your investment. As markets become more competitive, it's crucial to always compete on value, not price. I cannot stress this enough. By having better design, amenities, and photos, your listing will stay relevant for longer. You'll get a higher quantity of quality reviews, which will help you rank higher in search results and ultimately get more bookings year after year.

Let's look at an example. Assume you're all-in on a mountain house for $100,000. Your expected average daily rate is $300, and your occupancy rate is 60%, yielding a revenue of $65,700. Let's assume that after expenses and the mortgage, it's estimated that you will have a cash flow of $20,000 per year. That would equate to a 20% cash-on-cash return ($20,000 divided by $100,000).

You realize that the top properties near you, generating $80,000 or higher in revenue, all have a home theater room. If you can convert the garage into a theater room, you conclude that your average daily rate could increase to $350 and occupancy to 65%, yielding a revenue of $83,037 and boosting your annual cash flow to $37,337. On the other hand, it would cost you an extra $20,000 to convert the garage into a home theater room. This would bring your total investment to $120,000 instead of $100,000. The new expected COC return would be roughly 31% ($37,337 divided by $120,000), compared to the 20% COC return without the home theater room. In this case, since our COC return increased significantly, it would make sense to invest the extra money into adding the home theater room!

To recap, competing solely on price will always end up in a race to the bottom and diminishing returns. Instead, compete on value and focus on selling a compelling experience guests will have at your property. No matter how competitive a market gets, people will still travel there, and they will pay more money for the best possible experience. Executing on design, having great amenities, and professionally staged photos will help you get booked for a higher daily rate during the busy season and stay booked during the slow season when others simply do not.

CHAPTER SEVEN

Property Management

A t this point in the process, you have identified a market, selected a winning property, curated an irresistible design, packed your property full of amenities, and photographed it professionally. Now what? This is where the real fun begins. You need to set up your listing and build out the settings for your "tech stack": the software tools to help run the day-to-day operations. Before we dive into the systems, make sure you have applied for a short-term rental permit with the city you are located in, if applicable. Although this is a function of property management, I recommend doing this as soon as you acquire the property. Depending on the city, it can take days, or even weeks, to apply for and get approved for a permit. If you wait to do this until you are ready to rent, you will kick yourself. Most cities have short-term rental regulations and permit information readily available on their website. I recommend hopping on Google and searching: *"short-term rental permit [city name]."* In fact, you should be aware of the regulations and permitting process before you even begin evaluating properties in the first place!

Assuming you have your permit, let's move on to building your listing. I recommend building your listing on your preferred online travel agency (OTA) first and adding more OTAs later. For most people, this will be Airbnb. The process of creating a host profile and onboarding a new property is fairly self-explanatory, but I want to make a few key notes here.

First is your title. You have a limited number of characters, so you need to make the best use of the space. I like to think as if the traveler has to book a property without the ability to see photos or a description and they can only view the title of each property. What title tells the most attractive story about your property to a potential guest? Typically, I like to include keywords for amenities or the distance to the top local attraction(s). Sometimes I'll give the property a unique name, but not always. Nothing is permanent on your listing, and you can always come back and tweak things like your title to see what drives a higher ranking in search and more traction with travelers.

Nothing is more painful than reading titles of properties that make no sense, have no keywords, and tell me nothing about the property. For example, I just got on Airbnb and looked in Gatlinburg, where there are too many poor listings and bad property managers to count, and found a property titled *"Easy Living in Gatlinburg."* Another listing had the title *"Private Wooded Cabin Near Dollywood with Game Room."* (Dollywood is a large theme park nearby.) Which one of these listing titles is more appealing to you and drives more curiosity? I did the same search in Nashville, TN. One listing's title read *"Cozy Cottage in Prime Location."* Not very specific, and to those not familiar with Nashville, what does *"prime location"* mean, and is it actually a good location to rent? Another listing on the same page had the title *"2 Blks to Bdwy | Corner Condo | Gym | Pool | King."* Comparing these two titles, which ones are you more likely to click on and book? It helps to be specific and use keywords that travelers are searching for when booking a vacation in that market.

One mistake I see a lot of people make with their listing title is to state information that is already prevalent on Airbnb search results below their photo and title, like the number of bedrooms, the city, or the number of people they accommodate. These are the most common filters most people use when searching on Airbnb: location and number of guests. Don't be lazy. Get creative here and tell us as much as possible about your property that is not already a given based on search parameters travelers start with.

Second are your listing photos. We touched on this in the last chapter, but I want to really drive this point home and go a bit deeper. Your first photo is your cover photo and needs to be the highlight of your property. After all, that is the one photo that travelers can see when scrolling through hundreds of properties. Will it capture their attention, encourage them to click on your listing, and get them excited to learn more about it? A bad first photo is all it takes for someone to pass up on your listing and never click to learn more about it. The more times your listing shows up as a search impression and does not get clicked on, the lower it will appear in search as time goes on, resulting in fewer clicks and bookings.

When someone clicks on your listing, they're brought to your splash page, which is generally similar across all OTAs. On the splash page, you have five photos to showcase your property and garner enough interest to convince a traveler to scroll through all your photos and listing description. People are quick to say no, but it takes a while to give them the confidence to say yes and book your property. Your top five photos should highlight the top five selling points of your property. Showcase your top amenities, the location you're in, mountain or city views if you have them, any "wow" moments, etc. In other words, if somebody had access to only five photos and no other information about your property at all, what five photos would you choose to get them most interested in booking?

One of the most common mistakes I see hosts and property managers make is using the front of the house as the cover photo. For most listings, this is not going to capture someone's interest in your listing unless it's an especially beautiful house with noticeable amenities outside. Typically, a luxury property is the only time this would work. The next biggest mistake you can make with your splash page photos is to have them all showing various angles of the front of the house or of the living room, for example. This is not a listing on the MLS! Remember, you have but a few seconds to garner someone's full attention. Your job is to make it easy and quick for them to decide your property is the one.

Beyond your first five photos, make sure to continue showcasing the top highlights of your property first. Many property managers want to start with the front of the house, then move to all the photos of the living room, then the kitchen, then the bedrooms, then the bathrooms, then the game room, and then the outdoor spaces or backyard. I've scrolled through thousands of listings. All too often, I don't even realize that the property has a bad-ass game room, a hot tub in the backyard, a pool, or a fire pit until maybe the last 10 or 15 photos out of 50! To be honest, most travelers aren't going to scroll far enough in your photos to see them all, and they may not even realize you have these kinds of amenities unless you put them in the top section of your photos or in your listing title. They may very well write off your property after looking at the first five to ten photos and never even realize you have more to offer. They will exit your listing and keep searching for ones that have the amenities they are looking for. Make sure you order your photos properly to showcase the top amenities and your unique selling proposition for your property first.

If you have a larger property and feel that five photos are not enough to showcase what it has to offer, I would suggest trying a collage of four photos for your cover image, followed by the four next-best photos after that. When you're searching on a computer, most OTAs, like Airbnb, display the cover photo enlarged and about the same size as the next four photos combined. By creating a collage of four photos for your cover photo, your splash page appears to have eight photos of equal size instead of five. This allows you to show off more of your property right from the jump. When searching on your mobile device, clicking on a listing shows just the cover photo on the splash page. Utilizing a collage can be a great option, as this will get your top four photos on the splash page when searching on mobile instead of just one.

The third factor to pay attention to is your listing description and "space" description. The listing description on Airbnb has a character limit. You need to be concise and to the point, highlighting as much as you can about why somebody should book your place and the amenities you offer. Similarly to what we just covered for the title and photos, think as if you were a traveler, and you only had a listing description to read to decide if you want to book the property—no title or photos to look at. If the listing description was all the information provided to you as a traveler, would you have enough information to confidently book that property over others?

If people are visiting a market where the property location is crucial to what activities they will be doing, make sure to note the distance from those specific attractions here. For many of my listing descriptions, I use just one to three sentences describing the property, then use bullet points to highlight specific amenities or distances to local attractions. Using bullet points makes it easier for travelers to extract the info they need.

Remember, people have a short attention span! Beyond the description, you have a larger section called the "space" on Airbnb. This is where you should go into full detail about your property, all your amenities, the local area, and anything else that you can write to give your traveler full confidence that your property is the one. Most guests do not read this in its entirety, but some do. In this space, I describe each and every room and space on the property. Many novice hosts and property management companies fail to provide much detail here, and this hurts you in three ways.

First, as hosts, we want to eliminate as much unnecessary guest communication as possible. If a guest cannot find all the relevant information about your property and what their expectations should be by simply reading your listing description, they will ask you the silliest questions, costing you more time with day-to-day guest communication. Taking the time to write proper descriptions will save you countless hours responding to unnecessary guest questions and give guests more confidence to book faster without waiting on your responses.

Second, there may be something about your property that a guest does not know after reading the description, and the guest may make incorrect assumptions and ultimately book another accommodation where all the details of the property are made clear. People are lazy and like to avoid unnecessary conversation or friction when booking accommodations. Don't let this be the reason travelers do not book your property.

Third, when someone does book your property, it is critical to set clear expectations. Aside from an unclean property, nothing is more likely to get you a bad review than a guest who's upset because the listing did not accurately reflect the property. Being more descriptive in your listing description helps set proper expectations. For example, if a guest leaves you a bad review because your property has a shared backyard with a neighboring property, and they thought it was private, you can contest that review as long as your listing description accurately states that the backyard is indeed shared. However, if your backyard is shared and you fail to mention that in your listing, then it may turn into some negative reviews, which is the fastest way to harm your listing and ROI. Setting appropriate expectations will help you eliminate unnecessary guest communication and mitigate avoidable bad reviews.

Next, you need to make sure that your cancellation policy is selected and that you have a cleaning fee selected if you plan to charge one in addition to your daily rate (I'd recommend you do). Lastly, most OTAs, such as Airbnb and Vrbo, allow you to utilize a "new listing" discount, which is typically 20% off the first three reservations. I recommend taking advantage of this: it will boost your placement in search results and help you secure your first few bookings in a short period of time.

If your listing does not show up in search and does not get clicked on, you have zero chance of getting booked. In the long-term, on OTAs, you're going to need to pay attention to listing performance metrics or analytics, where you can view things such as search impressions, clicks on your listing, and, ultimately, conversions to actually get booked. If your analytics are good or improving, OTAs are likely to push you higher in their search results. In contrast, if you are showing up in search impressions but not getting clicked on, or getting clicked on but not getting booked, you will begin to appear lower in search results.

It's similar to a Google search. Google is trying to give you the results that help you get the answers you're looking for as quickly as possible. If someone searching on Google doesn't find what they're looking for, they may opt to try a different search engine. It's no different with OTAs. If someone is searching for a property to rent on Airbnb, and after a search where they had to dig into multiple pages of results and still didn't find what they are looking for, they might start searching on Vrbo, Booking.com, or begin searching for hotels. OTAs, therefore, use an algorithm to try and present properties that are most likely to be booked by the person searching based on their search criteria and filters. At the end of the day, all OTAs make money when people complete a reservation on their website, so they are incentivized to show each person exactly what they are looking for so they book quickly and more frequently. (We'll go into marketing in further detail a little later.)

Once you have at least one OTA set up, such as Airbnb, it's time to immediately set up your property management software of choice and sync it to your Airbnb account. There are many different property management software options on the market. Most of them do the same general tasks, allowing you to manage your rentals across multiple OTAs, all from one unified system. Property management software helps you automate day-to-day management tasks, such as guest messaging from a unified inbox. It enables you to schedule automated messages and message guests manually from one central location, regardless of the OTA. All your reservations will sync in one place, on one calendar, which helps you avoid being double-booked on two different OTAs for the same dates. You can even automate reviewing guests on certain platforms. If you choose to use a Wi-Fi-enabled smart lock, you can have your property management software change the codes for you between groups of guests and deliver the unique new code to the guest checking in. Property management software is non-negotiable if you want to run this business at scale on your own without creating a full-time job for yourself! As time goes on, property management software will only become more advanced and capable.

The most time-consuming part of setting up your property management software is building out your automated messages. This is crucial, so do not rush through this process! Like a great listing description, well-organized automated messages will clearly set expectations and eliminate unnecessary communication between guests before, during, and after each reservation. I recommend having, at minimum, the following automated messages built and scheduled for each reservation:

- *Reservation confirmation*, which is sent to any guest that completes a reservation, providing them with basic information about the property, when they can expect check-in instructions, etc.

- *Check-in instructions*, which I usually send out 48 hours prior to check-in time. This message gives the guest everything they need to know about the property: the access code to the front door, specific directions if it's not easily found on Google or Apple

Maps, and anything else that would be relevant and helpful prior to arriving.

- *House Rules*, which I personally like to send the day of check-in, to remind guests of anything specific they need to be aware of prior to arriving. This will include additional details about the property, all house rules, any idiosyncrasies about the property they need to know about, quiet hours, HOA or city rules, and fines for breaking the house rules.

- You can *send out a message the day after check-in* to see how things are going and ask if the guest needs anything in particular. This can be a nice touch of hospitality.

- *Checkout instructions* are sent 24 hours prior to checkout time. This will be a brief list of things the guest needs to do to checkout. Try to keep your checkout instructions short and to the point, without asking too much of the guest. This is the final impression a guest will have before checking out. The last thing you want is for them to feel overburdened with unnecessary house chores, which could leave a sour taste in their mouth and result in a negative review.

- Lastly, *a thank-you and review request message* is automatically sent the day after a guest checks out.

Property management software can even automate giving five-star reviews on platforms such as Airbnb to every single guest. If you want to do a manual review of something other than five stars, you're able to override this feature. Once you scale to multiple properties under management, any little monotonous task that you can automate, the better. After all, we are looking to create a more passive income stream, not another job for ourselves.

Once property management software is up and running, it's time to set up your dynamic pricing software. There are several dynamic pricing tools out there, and I'm sure more will be developed over time. At the time of writing this book, I personally recommend using either PriceLabs or Wheelhouse. The first thing to note here is that you should be connecting your dynamic pricing software directly to your property management software and not directly to the individual OTAs. The chain of command goes like this: PriceLabs dictates pricing and minimum night stay requirements and sends that information to your property management software on a daily basis. Your property management software then sends that information to all the OTAs associated with that specific property. A lot of individuals and property management companies make the mistake of not using dynamic pricing software at all and instead, deploy static pricing throughout the year or manually update pricing on their own. If you are not using dynamic pricing software, you are blindly walking past thousands of extra dollars per year in revenue and cash flow.

Static pricing means you charge the same flat rate every night of the year. In this case, you are missing out on a higher daily rate during peak-demand days, and you are also missing out on reservations when you are priced too high for the low-demand days. The two factors that determine how much revenue you generate with your property are your daily rate and occupancy. By leveraging dynamic pricing software, you can adjust the settings and make adjustments on the fly to maximize your occupancy at the highest daily rate possible, ultimately yielding the highest possible revenue.

Instead of charging a specific rate for weekends and another rate for weekdays, tools such as PriceLabs and Wheelhouse analyze data in the marketplace daily. They can tell when demand is higher or lower on any given day. When first setting up your customizations, it can seem overwhelming because there are so many different widgets you can choose from. Just remember that setting your pricing is not a "set it once and forget it" approach. It's a living and breathing system that requires consistent tweaks to get the most out of it. There are many different things that you can toggle on or off to set various parameters for the software to dictate your price each day. However, having more settings toggled on does not necessarily equate to more accurate pricing. Most dynamic pricing solutions look at your base rate, make adjustments based on your customizations, and ultimately change the price dynamically up or down based on the demand they are seeing for any given day.

This is why it is called "dynamic pricing software," not static pricing software. Dynamic pricing software will pick up on trends or information that you may not even know about in your market. For example, if there is an event like a concert or sporting event coming to your city, there is likely going to be an increase in demand for those specific days. Hotels and other properties around you are all going to increase their pricing accordingly. However, if you have static pricing, someone could book your property at a cheaper price before you even realize there is an event on those specific dates. On the flip side, let's say you get booked on all the weekends but rarely get weekday bookings. Don't just assume that people only travel on weekends and your property can't get booked during the weekdays. I see properties in markets I operate in making $10,000–$30,000 less than mine per year, not because mine is a better property, but simply because they are priced too high for low-demand days such as weekdays. This is different in each market, but midweek travelers are typically more price-conscious than weekend travelers.

Most dynamic pricing software will allow you to compare your pricing to competitors in the market. This is a crucial tool to leverage. If you are not getting many bookings, take a look at the competitive analysis chart, and you will likely quickly figure out that it's due to your property being overpriced compared to your competitors. Conversely, you might be super happy that your occupancy is through the roof but may not realize that you are leaving money on the table on many days throughout the year. By looking at this chart, you'll quickly be able to analyze if you can adjust your customizations to increase pricing and achieve a higher daily rate without lowering your occupancy rate. The goal is to find the right balance between daily rates and occupancy to achieve the highest possible revenue. Having this information at your fingertips is priceless.

Many hosts and property management companies are stubborn when it comes to pricing and simply won't go below a certain price because they believe their property should be booked at a specific rate. The result? Days get left unbooked, and occupancy and revenue ultimately suffer. This also hurts your ranking in search results, which will lead to fewer bookings and demand for your property over time. Your pricing strategy needs to be tweaked and adjusted consistently. If your property is not priced correctly, you may not show up in search results at all. And if you do, travelers may scroll right past your listing because it is out of their price range for the days they are looking at. As we noted above, if guests see your listing (search impression) but never click on it, or they click on it but never book, it will hurt your ranking in search results long-term.

When you first launch your listing, it can take several weeks—or even months—to fully ramp up in order to optimize search ranking placement, establish reviews, and optimize booking lead time to hit your forecasted revenue target. This leads me to my next point, which is how you can outperform 90% of properties in your market: the short-term rental perpetual lifecycle.

Your property has great amenities, terrific design, impeccable photos, a clear title and description, a large number of five-star reviews, and is accurately priced. If you have all these elements dialed in, you will start to fill your calendar with more reservations. The more reservations you get, the higher the quantity of quality reviews you will receive. When future guests are evaluating your property compared to others, and they see limited availability on your calendar paired with a ton of five-star reviews, they will begin to associate value with your property, and they are more likely to book at that premium rate. This starts a cycle that will lead to more bookings, more reviews, higher search results ranking, more search impressions, more clicks, more bookings, repeat. This is what I call the "short-term rental perpetual lifecycle," and once you hit a stride, you can really maximize the revenue and, ultimately, the cash flow of your property.

In order to maximize revenue, we need to hone in on a near-perfect pricing strategy. I could dedicate an entire chapter to pricing strategies, so here, I'll cover some of the most important things that will have the biggest impact. First and foremost, before you even acquire a property, you should have a keen understanding of what you think you should be charging per night throughout the year. You should know the difference in what you'll be charging on weekends versus weekdays.

When you first fire up your dynamic pricing software, you need to first pick an appropriate base price. Once you do this, check how the software prices your property throughout the next 12 months. You can look at your comp set and see if you are priced accurately, too low, or too high. Adjust accordingly until you feel the base price accurately reflects the pricing you want on your calendar. Based on your findings, you will then select the customizations you'd like to turn on. Your customizations will be various things you can turn on or off to optimize your pricing or minimum night stay requirements to yield the highest level of booking performance. You can change things such as weekend vs. weekday pricing minimums, premiums or discounts, last-minute discounts and far-out premiums, and specific day-of-week adjustments. You can change your minimum night stay requirements based on booking lead time.

For example, for anything outside of 90 days, you could have a five-night minimum stay, but for anything under 90 days, you want your minimum night stay to be only three nights. You have the ability to create your own seasons, so your base price, minimum and maximum price, and minimum night stay profiles are different according to specified periods during the year. Remember, we are trying to have our pricing be as accurate as possible to get booked for as many days possible at the highest daily rate. The days of setting the same daily rate for the entire year are over, and you will get crushed by the competition if you do that.

Since there is no "one size fits all" pricing strategy, you will need to toggle these customizations until you feel like your pricing is dialed in enough that you don't have to make many changes going forward. When you first launch a new listing, continue to tweak pricing each week until you get a nice flow of reservations coming in. If you feel like you are getting too many reservations (yes, I know that sounds crazy, but it's possible), start to push your pricing up little by little. If you are not getting booked enough, lower your prices slightly each week until you figure out what the market demands for your property are and bookings start to fill the calendar.

As time goes on, you will know your listing and what prices you get booked at better than anyone else. One key thing to watch and take notes on over time is your booking lead time. You can find this in the Airbnb insights tab or directly inside most property management software analytics tabs. Booking lead time is how many days in advance, on average, your property gets booked.

For example, if you have 100 bookings this year and, on average, your guests are booking 30 days in advance, your average booking lead time is 30 days. Why is this so important? You use this to understand when your pricing needs to be most in line with market demand—when guests are most likely to search for and book your property. Assuming your property's booking lead time is exactly 30 days, I suggest applying a slight premium to your prices for bookings more than 40 days in advance. For bookings under 30 days, I recommend implementing a gradual discount. As the booking lead time shortens toward a same-day booking, your pricing discount should gradually increase.

A huge mistake I see a lot of hosts and property managers make is setting a floor to their pricing that is too high. While you might think your property shouldn't be getting booked at anything less than $500/night, this doesn't mean you will get every day booked at that price. On weekends, you'll likely get booked at or above your expected average daily rate. But for weekdays or during the slow season, it's important to get as aggressive as necessary to maximize the number of bookings, reviews, and occupancy. Remember the short-term perpetual lifecycle! This will only help you in the long run. If you are priced too high, especially for weekdays or the slow season, you will start to get demoted in search result rankings, which will hurt you not just in the slow season but also as demand ramps up during the busy season.

After you secure your first three "new listing discount" reservations, I suggest lowering your pricing a good bit to begin filling your calendar. Since you don't have any reviews yet and you are not yet ranking high in OTA search results, it's important to compete more on price early on simply to drive traffic to your listing. It takes most listings some time to get fully ramped up. Nothing helps boost your listing in search result rankings quicker than adjusting the price. Once you hit a good stride, your calendar begins to fill up, and booking lead time is established, you can start to creep pricing up. A big mistake new short-term rental operators make is pricing too high when they first list, but reservations are slow to come in because the listing has yet to become established.

Here's a pro tip on pricing strategy that I want to share with you, which will help you make thousands more per year than the average host would make with that same property. This works especially well in urban markets. Once you have weekends booked, I suggest lowering the prices significantly on the midweek gap days, especially if the booking lead time is less than your average. Lower them as much as necessary to get as many bookings as possible in order to maximize your occupancy. Most hosts are happy with weekend bookings and will likely still have ample cash flow. What they don't understand is that they are missing out on an extra $1,000 or $2,000 or more per month in cash flow simply by getting more weekdays booked. This strategy works incredibly well in urban markets where there is always a flurry of midweek travelers who are more price-conscious when booking.

An average daily rate is just that—an average, not the rate at which you expect every night to get booked. Some nights will be booked at a much higher rate, and some will be booked at a much lower rate. By lowering the prices drastically to attract midweek bookings, especially last-minute bookings, you can pad your revenue by hundreds, if not thousands, of dollars per month for days that you'd likely not get booked at all if you didn't lower your prices in the first place. The weekend traveler is typically willing to pay for the experience at a premium rate, while the midweek traveler is usually more price-conscious and has more supply to choose from since, in most markets, midweek occupancy is lower than on weekends. By getting more reservations, you are not only increasing your revenue, but you are also going to drastically increase the number of positive reviews you get. The more you get booked and the higher quantity of positive reviews you have, the higher you will rank in search results. Again, this leads back to the short-term rental perpetual lifecycle. Don't let your ego get the best of you on pricing your property: it will cost you thousands of dollars per year.

The other benefit of lowering your price for midweek gap days is that it will make the total cost to the traveler seem lower than the competition. Keep in mind, if you are charging a cleaning fee of $100 and your daily rate is $100, and a guest books your property for a one-night stay, the total cost to them before taxes and fees is $200 per night. If that same guest books your property at $100 per night for five nights with a $100 cleaning fee, the total cost to the guest is $600, or $120 per night. That's a big difference! This is why I lower pricing for gap days. It makes pricing more competitive and attractive compared to the competition. Most property managers and hosts fail to recognize that this is priced too high and ultimately struggle to fill one to two-day gaps.

Once you have your listing set up on the OTA of your choice, your property management software connected, and your dynamic pricing dialed in, I would start to list your property on other OTAs, such as Vrbo, Booking.com, etc.

You'll also need to consider cleaning and maintenance. Before we dive into how to automate the cleaning and turnover management, let's discuss the criteria for a cleaning company for a short-term rental. I recommend interviewing cleaners at least two weeks before you plan to stage and photograph your property. This way, you can schedule a deep clean the day before photos to ensure the property is immaculate. There are several ways to find cleaners. The best cleaners I have used have typically come from word of mouth, recommended by somebody I network with, such as a realtor, another investor who owns property locally, a lender, etc. At the time of writing this book, Turno is the main software application I use and recommend for turnover management. Turno is also a marketplace for cleaners and hosts to meet and transact business. Hosts can post a property and job listing on Turno, and cleaners can apply for it with a suggested cleaning rate. Another way to find cleaners is by posting in local Facebook groups or posting a job listing on

Indeed or a similar website. When interviewing cleaners, asking questions and setting clear expectations is critical for a successful relationship. The following topics or questions must be addressed:

- The cleaner must charge a specified rate per turn and not charge an hourly rate.

- The cleaner must be able to do same-day turns (a guest checks out in the morning, and a new guest checks in that afternoon).

- Do they provide linens, or do you?

- Do they do laundry on-site or off-site?

- Is the same team of individual cleaners cleaning the property each turn?

- What is their quality control process?

- What is the process for cleaners to report damage, maintenance issues, etc.?

- Do they also provide any preventative maintenance packages or handyman services? If not, do they know or recommend any local handymen?

- How do they prefer to invoice and be paid?

- Do they currently use software like Turno? If not, are they open to using it?

- How do they stay up to date with reservations and ensure no turns get missed? They must use something like Turno, Resort Cleaning, or other software. If they ask to be added as a co-host or for you to send screenshots of your bookings, it's a recipe for missed cleans and more communication than necessary.

- Do they replace small things like burnt-out light bulbs, batteries in remotes, propane tanks, etc.? Is that included in their cost or extra?

- Do they keep track of inventory of items such as towels, paper products, and other items provided to guests? If yes, what system do they use to track inventory?

- Do they restock items such as toilet paper, paper towels, cleaning supplies for guests, etc.? What is the process for this? Is there an extra cost? Do they order and purchase these items, or do I send them to the property when they tell me it's time to order?

- What is their communication style and preference (text, call, etc.)? Must communicate well.

- Do they take before and after photos of the entire property each clean? This is important, as you need evidence anytime a guest damages or leaves a place trashed when filing a claim for reimbursement. It also ensures accountability and consistency with your cleaners.

- How many other short-term rentals do they clean? How long have they been cleaning short-term rentals? Do they do other types of real estate or focus solely on short-term rentals?

- How big is their team currently? Do they have the bandwidth to take on new properties?

- What happens if a guest checks in and something was missed by the cleaning staff? How do they remediate these issues in a timely manner?

Once you have selected a cleaning company, it's time to connect your property management software to the turnover management software of your choice. There are multiple different turnover and cleaning management software options out there, but the two that I recommend at the time of writing this book are Turno and Resort Cleaning. If you are sending screenshots of reservations to your cleaners or texting them every day to make sure they know when to clean your properties, you're going to be wasting a lot of your time. Turnover management software will not only help you—it'll also make your cleaner's business run smoother!

Turnover management software will notify your cleaners when you get a new reservation or when one is canceled. They will be able to peer into your calendar and view all upcoming reservations. You can provide a cleaning checklist or protocols for your specific property for them to follow and keep an inventory of specific items. This will save you and your cleaner a great deal of unnecessary communication and allow you to focus your time on more important matters. Ensuring your cleaners have accurate reservation information will help mitigate any chances of a missed clean. A missed clean can be detrimental, and if it happens and it's not fixed immediately, you're likely going to have to refund your guests, and it will cost you a bad review. Avoidable refunds and bad reviews will crush you as a host.

Your cleaners are going to be your biggest asset. Establishing proper lines of communication from the start is critical. Your cleaners should be notifying you of any damage to the property. When damage occurs, or there is a maintenance problem, you will need a good handyman or maintenance service. Having both great cleaners and a great handyman will allow you to manage short-term rentals anywhere in the world, not just in the local market where you live.

In some markets, cleaning companies will also have a maintenance branch or at least have maintenance contacts. If you find a way to automate the maintenance and have the cleaners report directly to the maintenance team, you will save yourself some future headaches and a ton more time. Cleaning and maintenance issues cause 99% of bad guest reviews. The two things guests complain about the most and ask for refunds for are if the property is not cleaned to their expectations or if some functionality of the property is not meeting their expectations as depicted in the listing. If you can prevent these issues from happening in the first place, you are setting yourself up for a lot of five-star reviews.

If you set up your systems and software tools properly, self-managing short-term rentals should take you no more than 30 to 60 minutes per week, per property, on average. Self-managing is not for everyone, though. If you have a job that does not give you the flexibility to be responsive to guests in a pinch, you may want to consider hiring a virtual assistant, co-host, or property management company. Or, if you have scaled beyond a certain point and are tired of self-managing and want it to be completely passive income, it might be a good time to evaluate a property manager.

I encourage you to self-manage when first starting out. Most PMs charge 15%–30% of the gross or net accommodation fare. Self-managing will save you this, and you can reinvest it into more properties quicker. For example, if you have a property that brings in $100,000 per year in revenue, you'd be giving up $15,000–$30,000 for something that, if set up correctly, will only take you about an hour per week to manage yourself. Now imagine if you had ten of those properties doing $100,000 each per year. That would be a million dollars of revenue per year, meaning you would be giving up $250,000 per year to management if their fee was 25%. There does come a point in time where you will have to hire VAs or employees to help run the day-to-day management, or else it will ultimately become a full-time job once you scale to a certain number of properties. I'd recommend either hiring help or outsourcing to a good property manager once you are above five to eight properties, depending on the workload.

For some investors, it makes sense to outsource property management out of the gate. Let's face it: if you are an emergency room doctor and can't have access to your phone for several hours at a time, it will become challenging to self-manage properties. Plus, you are going to be better off treating this like a formal business. At some point, you will want to spend your time working on the business and not in the business. This means taking yourself out of the day-to-day management so you can strategically focus on growing your investment portfolio.

That being said, if you decide to outsource management to a property management company, they must have a track record of bringing in as much or higher revenue for properties than other operators locally. They should be using all the types of software I mentioned above and more. They should also be listed on multiple OTAs and have a direct booking website with a real marketing strategy. If they are solely taking bookings on a direct booking website but do not list on popular OTAs such as Airbnb or Vrbo, you should likely refrain from working with them, as they'll be limiting the visibility of your properties to travelers. You want your property manager to provide full-service management as well. After all, if they are charging you 15%–30% of revenue, they better be making this a passive stream of income for you!

One thing I will caution you about is that a 20% property management fee doesn't always mean the same thing. First, always ask your property manager if the 20% is being charged on the gross or net amount of each reservation. If they charge on the gross amount, it may include the accommodation rate, cleaning fee, taxes, and other applicable fees. Whereas if they were charging on the net amount, it would likely be just a percentage of the accommodation rate. This is a stark difference between the two.

Second, look at some of their existing listings on OTAs. Are they charging guests a large management fee on top of the accommodation rate and cleaning fee? I have seen both big and small property management companies charging as high as 10%–15% accommodation rate in the form of management fees to the guest on top of the normal management rate they charge you. They are basically double-dipping. I don't blame them— they will make more money with each reservation—but it can be detrimental to your listing and your profitability. If the property manager is charging an extra 10%–15% to the guest on OTAs, the properties that directly compete with yours, priced the same per night and without a management fee, will get booked nearly 100% of the time before your property does since the overall price to the guest is 10%–15% lower.

When selecting a property management company, make sure they're hyper-focused on revenue management, and transparent with property owners about their fees.

I co-founded Home Team Vacation Rentals with one of my first-ever BNB Investor Academy students, Elliott Caldwell. Our mission is simple: maximize revenue and cash flow for our homeowners while providing unparalleled experiences for guests from around the world. We leverage a variety of software tools to help us effectively and sustainably grow our business. We consistently outperform the market averages we operate in because we run each of our properties under management as if they were our own investment. Home Team Vacation Rentals is the only property management company I can wholeheartedly recommend at this point in time, because I know things are done the right way.

If you want to learn more about Home Team Vacation Rentals or schedule an intro call with our team, please scan the QR code, go to www.hometeamvr.com or check us out on social media @hometeamvacationrentals.

Let's talk about a direct booking strategy. I recommend building a direct bookings website if you plan to host yourself long-term, have a high concentration of properties in one market, or plan to build a property management business. However, if you plan to outsource management within the next few years, a direct booking site may not be worth your time and effort. The reason I say that is because getting direct bookings is not a short-term strategy. It is a long-term game, and it takes time to gradually increase the number of direct bookings you get. The main way to secure more direct bookings is by building up an email list. The best leads for future direct bookings are people who have already stayed at one of your properties. Hopefully, they had such a great experience, and they are willing to rent from you again the next time they visit and recommend your property to friends and family. So, how do you get them to book directly instead of booking on one of the OTAs?

You can put signage in your property with a QR code saying something like *"Book direct and save."* If you have multiple properties, it can say *"Check out our other properties, book direct and save."* To secure direct bookings, you need a good marketing strategy. One of the best ways to market is via email. First, you'll need to build an email list by collecting emails from every single person who enters your home. There are a few ways to do this. You can leverage software such as StayFi, which requires each person in every group that rents your property to enter their name and email to access the Wi-Fi. This is very similar to a hotel, where a guest checks in, and every single person needs to exchange their contact info to connect to the Wi-Fi. The more emails you collect, the more people you can market to. And the bigger your portfolio grows, the more properties you'll be able to market to that email list.

The reason direct bookings are a long-term game is that you should not expect to get an extraordinarily large number of direct bookings in the first year or two, especially if you just have one or a few properties. As time goes on, your email list will grow, and your direct bookings will grow with it. You may be asking yourself, *Why bother with direct bookings when it's so easy to just list on OTAs like Airbnb?* First of all, you have very little control over your reservations made through an OTA. You also make less money through OTAs, which makes sense because these companies have built amazing platforms for you to list your property for rent and do the marketing for you. They have to make their money somehow. But, with direct bookings, you are going to keep a lot more of the revenue since you eliminate the OTA fee for both you as the host and the guest!

For example, at the time of writing this book, Airbnb charges around 3% to hosts and around 12% to guests. This means that you could ultimately give the guest a 5% discount by booking directly and still make 10% higher revenue per booking. This makes the guest happy and will certainly make you happy. For starters, you can build a simple direct booking website using most property management software's in-house website builder. However, long term, you'll likely want to work with an agency or hire someone to build a more formal direct booking website that is not directly affiliated with the property management software and can run independently. You can integrate your direct booking software with your property management software so everything is integrated seamlessly.

Since you are treating these investments as a business, you need to have proper bookkeeping as well. Why is this so important? Well, for one, it is critical that you understand your rental income, expenses, and, ultimately, your monthly and annual profits. Secondly, and more importantly, you need to keep a clean record of your books so that when it comes time to file taxes and work with a CPA, you don't have to spend countless hours getting them the information they need. Organization is key here. Also, in the case of an audit from the IRS, documentation is everything. It all starts with proper bookkeeping. It may not seem like a big deal when first starting out, and you have just one property, but as you scale, it is important you have all your systems and processes dialed in. The longer you wait, the more painful it will be to retroactively fix poor bookkeeping.

For bookkeeping itself, I recommend using something like QuickBooks. I started using a spreadsheet that I custom-built. However, as with anything that requires manual entries, it inevitably leads to more unintentional errors over time. I moved over to QuickBooks after the first year in business. As you scale, the more you can automate with software, the better. This is why I recommend using bookkeeping software right from the start. If you are using QuickBooks, you can even give access to your CPA to simplify things during tax season and, yet again, save yourself countless hours of unnecessary work.

CHAPTER EIGHT

Taking Action and Scaling

A ll of this information is useless unless you take action. I can't tell you how many people I meet who seem to know everything about real estate. That's all they talk about, yet they don't have a single investment property to show for it. What good is all the information just sitting in your brain if not applied in practice? Most people fail to ever take the first step. You will miss 100% of the shots you don't take! The first step is always the most daunting because you typically think of the entire process and get so overwhelmed you end up doing nothing at all. It's no different than setting the goal of getting in great physical shape. You do all the research online, download all the workout plans, find a diet to follow, and you feel more prepared than ever. Yet the hardest part is simply getting out of bed in the morning, getting yourself dressed, hopping in the car, and driving to the gym on that first day. It's the same thing when it comes to investing in real estate and short-term rentals. The hardest part is getting started and taking the leap of faith. If you commit to taking action, follow the processes detailed in this book, and execute on your vision, you have a very high chance of success with short-term rentals. If you are one of the ambitious people who read this book and actually take action, I commend you!

Once you have your first short-term rental under your belt, it's time to start thinking bigger. Remember the three stages of financial freedom we talked about earlier? You'll get to Stage 1 financial freedom before you know it. But once you are there, don't stop! You need to formalize a plan to get to Stage 2 and, ultimately, Stage 3 financial freedom—you remember, having *fuck you money*, but in a good way.

In order to get to stage one, financial freedom, we need to have enough monthly cash flow to cover our living expenses. What is the monthly cash flow you currently need to achieve this? From here, you just need to work backward. If your answer is $6,000 per month, then you just need three short-term rental properties that cash flow $2,000 per month each or six properties that cash flow $1,000 per month each. You can do the math. You can accomplish this using one or multiple strategies discussed in this book. If you are buying properties, you will eventually want to scale faster than your investable capital allows. This doesn't mean you have to stop and wait to save up for another down payment. Instead, I'd encourage you to do the following: partner with other investors who have money, pursue rental arbitrage, or start a co-hosting or property management business. Don't pigeonhole yourself into thinking the only strategy that you can do is buying on your own, with your own capital. BNB Investor Academy students who have scaled the fastest have deployed multiple different strategies simultaneously.

I've met hundreds of people who took years to start and even longer to scale to substantial cash flow because they were too narrow-minded and only wanted to buy on their own. I personally used to think like this, and I regret it. The faster you can scale your overall cash flow, the faster you can start to reinvest and grow your portfolio, the faster you will become financially free, and the faster you will accumulate wealth. I have also met many people who have a large real estate portfolio yet have never invested a dime of their own money! Leveraging other people's money (OPM) is how some of the biggest real estate investors of all time got started and scaled. If they can do it, so can you.

As we turn the final page of this journey together, I extend a heartfelt invitation to you: if this book has sparked even a single insight or inspiration in your heart, I humbly ask for a moment of your time—a mere two minutes—to share your experience in an online review. Your words will not only mean the world to me but also have the power to guide others on their path to financial independence.

Imagine the ripple effect your recommendation could create. Share this book with a friend, a family member, or introduce it to your followers on social media with a snapshot and a tag to @melefante6. Your action could be the beacon that lights another's way to financial freedom.

This book aims to lay the groundwork for you to embark on and expand your journey in short-term rentals, aspiring to unlock financial freedom for you at an early age. Understanding that the road to independence is unique for each individual and knowing that some may seek further guidance, I extend an invitation to those who wish to accelerate their journey. At BNB Investor Academy, my team and I offer personalized coaching and mentorship to navigate the complexities of short-term rentals. Our mission has empowered thousands toward financial liberation in as little as one to two years.

Visit us at www.bnbinvestoracademy.com, scan the QR code or reach out on Instagram @melefante6 to explore how we can tailor our expertise to your aspirations.

We offer a comprehensive coaching experience, complete with all the tools, resources, templates, and a vibrant community to support your growth.

Let's not let this book be the end of our conversation. Whether our paths merge through further collaboration or not, I'd love to hear from you. Share your thoughts on the book, your milestones, or when you launch your first short-term rental. Reach out on Instagram—I'm here to listen and support.

Remember, your potential is limitless. You possess the strength to make your dreams a reality. Whenever doubt whispers, counter it with a powerful question: *"Why not me?"*

Together, let's open the door to the future you deserve.

THANK YOU FOR READING MY BOOK!

Thank you for reading my book! Here are a few free bonus resources.

Scan the QR Code Here:

I appreciate your interest in my book and value your feedback as it helps me improve future versions of this book. I would appreciate it if you could leave your invaluable review on Amazon.com with your feedback. Thank you!

Made in United States
Troutdale, OR
12/10/2024

26254262R10070